Thank you may you be prosper!

The 40-Day Financial Fast

Shifting Your Paradigm toward Financial Freedom

Pastor D. L. Williams

Printed in the United States of America.

First Printing: October 2017

ISBN-13: 978-0-692-91654-4

Dedication

I would like to dedicate this book to my lovely wife, Precious Williams, who always encouraged me to write a book. Who woke up one morning and shared her dream of seeing me on a stage talking about a book that I had written, and who always saw an author in me before I even saw it in myself. To my mother, Sheila Williams, who gave me my first book on finances, in which helped me to begin understanding how money works, and helped me with starting to get my financial life together. To my children, Deshaun, Katelynn, Kristian, Kristin, Aiden, Harrison, & Langston, who collectively inspire me to work hard and be as great as I have the potential to be, and to leave a legacy that they can all follow with pride. I pray that this book leads to you all adopting a mindset of wealth, and to you all not only passing down generational wealth, but also principles of wealth to my grandchildren, my great grandchildren, and those who follow my bloodline.

~ D.L.Williams, M.Div.

Table of Contents

Introduction

Usually, when it comes to fasting, we are asked to give up ordinary pleasures like meat, sweets, bread, drinks, or nowadays even social media for 21 to 40 days. Whatever we are asked to abstain from, the overall purpose is to subject our flesh-driven desires and then feed our spiritual man more intentionally. Fasting is a time of self-denial, a time of self-sacrifice. It's a time when we deny ourselves some of our most routine everyday desires in order to become more spiritually synched.

From ancient times, fasting has always been considered a period when we purposefully take control of our flesh and deny it the authority to control us and our individual decisions. We refuse to let our flesh compel us to indulge in everything it feels it must have to survive. However, we all know that the things we think we must have are things that we really don't necessarily "have to have."

Fasting is a spiritual practice used in combination with prayer to realign ourselves with God. And isn't it true that in the course of time, our spiritual life gets lost, weakened, and very much so misaligned? We can become so lopsided and distorted spiritually that it greatly affects many aspects of our natural lives negatively—and we don't even know it.

This is why I am so glad you have decided to go on this new journey with me. When we get out of line spiritually, it not only adversely affects our relationships, character, business, occupation, ministries, future plans, and present accomplishments, but it also can have an undesirable impact on our finances.

Financial stewardship is spiritually important, even for those who are not Christians or believers in God. But particularly for us as citizens of the kingdom of God, how we handle our finances is even more significant. It's vital because the way we manage our wealth should ultimately bring glory to God and be a reflection of our faith. This is not just limited to the tithe! Yes, offering the tithe (10% of our income) honors God according to the Scriptures, but the way we manage the remainder of our money (our 90%) should equally honor Him as well. What sense does it make to honor God with the tithe, but then turn right around and disgrace Him with the way we handle the rest of our finances—operating in greed, lack of generosity, discontentment, debt, wastefulness, financial carelessness, and rambunctious living?   Honoring Him with the tithe, but then dishonoring Him with the way we use our 90% to satisfy our financial addictions.

Just as our flesh can become dependent on things that it feels it has to have, such as food, alcohol, sex, and drugs, it can also become addicted to uncontrollable spending, resulting in terrible financial habits. The spirit of greed, wanting to *gain it all* and keep up with the Joneses, has created unnecessary financial strain on many of us today. Being greedy simply means to chase after or seek to indulge in what we don't *need.* And we do so because we have psychologically conditioned ourselves into believing "we just got to have it." This happens when we haven't learned the art of being content, which is a very significant Christian discipline to have.

Luke 12:15 (NIV) says, "Be on your guard against all kinds of greed; life does not consist in an abundance of possessions." The Message Bible says, "Protect yourself from the least bit of greed. Life is not defined by what you have, even when you have a lot." Jesus Christ's instructions advise us to protect ourselves from being materialistic and greedy because having things is *not* what life is all about.

According to the Word of God, the best way to protect ourselves against greed is by following the advice of Paul to Timothy in 1 Timothy 6:6. Paul says, "There is great gain in godliness with contentment; for we brought nothing into this world, and we will take nothing out of it. But if we have food and clothing, with these we need to be content. But those who desire to be rich fall into temptation, into a trap, into many *senseless and hurtful desires* that plunge men into *ruin and destruction.*" In other words, we all need to learn how to be satisfied with what we have and live without some things, or else our greed for more will destroy us.

It is my belief that the number-one reason so many people are in terrible financial straits right now is that they simply have not grasped the spiritual discipline of contentment, which is the reason this book will be a tremendous blessing for your financial life. You are about to embark upon a journey of self-discovery and transformation. This fast will help you align your stewardship practices with God's will, challenge you to be more fiscally responsible, detox you from being a constant consumer, deliver you from self-indulgence, and recondition you to produce wealth as God has given you the ability to do.

Financial Freedom

Most people don't understand the phrase, "financial freedom." The majority of the younger generation don't even talk about attaining it, while many in the older generation have given up on it. But it's never too early or late to work towards being financially free.

In a nutshell, financial freedom means being delivered from paycheck dependence. It's the ability to live life on your terms and do the things you really want to do without having to worry about money. Financial freedom involves making typical life decisions unconstrained by money or the lack thereof—such as taking a few days off to go visit with family members you haven't seen in a while or attend homecoming to see all of your college friends, hit a few day parties, and have a good time. Ask yourself how many things have you missed out on that you really wanted to do but didn't do, or places that you really wanted to go but didn't go simply because you couldn't afford to miss a couple of days of work and have your paycheck come up short. Perhaps you couldn't afford to pay a sitter to keep your children for the number of days you wanted to be away. Or, you just simply didn't have the money.

Let me ask you a series of questions that will give you an idea of just how financially free you are right now today. Considering the amount of money that's in your checking and savings accounts right now at this very moment, what would happen if you did not get your next paycheck? Could you pay all of your bills before the due dates? Buy groceries? Take care of an unexpected emergency costing from $300 to $500? Get two full tanks of gas? Catch a newly released movie with friends and stop by the concession stand for soda and popcorn? Get your hair cut or your nails done? If you could answer yes to all of these questions, you are financially free by *at least* one paycheck. If you answered no to any of these questions, you are not financially free at all! What if you missed your next two paychecks? What if you didn't get paid for a month? Six months? A year?

What I'm trying to help you understand here is just how close you are to seeing your life become drastically different from what it is now with regular paychecks coming in. The reality is that you just paused and realized the ugly truth—that you are no more than one to three paychecks away from being homeless! Isn't that a scary reality to face? You are only seven to 21 days away from moving back in with your parent(s), sleeping in your car, crashing on a friend's pull-out couch, calling a homeless shelter to see if they've got room for just one more, asking for someone else's leftovers, or sleeping outside on a park bench. Stop for a second. Go online right now, check your account balances, and read that last statement again. You are only a paycheck or two away from your life being drastically different from what it is right now!

So now that you realize it, how do you change it? Good question. You need to start working towards financial freedom *today*. Not tomorrow, today! Get your mind set on the goal of

11

attaining paycheck independence. You can do it! Financial freedom can be achieved for all of us if we understand where we are and where we're trying to get to, and then employ the discipline, diligence and persistence it takes to get there.

We can reach this goal called financial freedom, but we must first break the chains of this consumerism mentality. We have to change our concept of wealth and deprogram our minds from thinking that owning luxury cars, the latest technological inventions, designer clothes, name-brand shoes, and other materialistic goods is the real measurement of wealth and even self-worth. We must change our mindset to measure wealth simply by how much financial freedom we truly need to live the life we want to live. That's the real wealth indicator.

It's not about a certain dollar amount. You don't need to have a million dollars in the bank to be wealthy. Wealth is a subjective matter that is dependent upon the life an individual person desires to live. Some people don't need a million dollars to be wealthy, because even though having that amount of money is impressive to have, it's not necessary for the life they desire to live. For them, having a mere $100,000 in their savings makes them wealthy and financially free because it's a suitable amount for the life they aspire to live.

What about you? What kind of life do you want to live? What do you need financially to be totally free to live that life without depending on a paycheck? How long you can stay independent of a paycheck—whether it's a work paycheck, an alimony check, a retirement check, a child support check, or a royalty check—before you have to drastically change the way you truly want to live is the real extent of your wealth and measurement of your financial freedom. I don't know about you, but I still have a whole lot of work to do, because I'm nowhere near as financially free as I truly want to be!

Aha Moment

In 2008 I was called to pastor my very first church in a small city in Illinois named Danville, where I served until December of 2013. I had lived in a few different cities prior to going to Danville, and I must say it wasn't one of my most favorite places. As a native of Mobile, Alabama, who also lived in places like Atlanta, I was more accustomed to warm weather during the year. In the Deep South, we had warm to blazing hot weather at least seven months out of the year. Snow, to us, was miracle weather—like manna falling from heaven! We would get a dusting of snow once every seven years or so. Even then, it was only a few centimeters, but still enough to shut the entire city down. Not in Danville! There, it gets cold in October, starts snowing in November, and continues snowing until April. Unlike the place I was from, seven months out of the year were cold. Ironically, seven is the number of completion, and living in Danville was *the complete opposite* of what I was accustomed to.

On one particular day in Danville that just so happened to be warm, I was riding the streets of the city heading to my church office. At the time, I owned a white C230 Mercedes Benz with tinted windows and a biscuit-color interior. It was nice. I was proud of that car because it was the first one I had ever purchased. I was listening to the radio, riding with the windows down. For some reason, I was checking out a talk show that just so happened to be on, and they

14

were discussing finances. What I heard that day changed the way I handled my money for the rest of my life! I forget the name of the guest on the show, but he was an African-American man. He made one statement that I will never forget because it changed my perception about finances. He simply said, "The average black person can't get their hands on $1,000 of their own money at any given moment (not including credit cards)."

He continued to talk about how the African-American community, as descendants of slavery and Jim Crow, have been denied possessions for so long simply because we were black and considered "less than" our white peers. Because of this, we have become financially fixated on possessing things in order to authenticate ourselves and find some type of meaning for our existence. So now we live in big houses, wear expensive clothing, and drive Cadillacs, Beamers, and Benzes, thinking that by doing this we validate or even increase our personal value. But even though we live in those nice houses, wear those designer clothes, and drive those luxury vehicles, we can't even get our hands on $1,000 of our own money if we were asked to do so.

Let me tell you, I was confronted, convicted, and converted all at the same time because this radio guest was talking about *me*! As I was riding in my white, tinted-window C230 Benz with the biscuit-colored interior, I was immediately met head on with the bitter reality that I couldn't get my hands on a meager $1,000. This was a most embarrassing yet enlightening moment for me. Even though I was mortified both by my ignorance to think that something as immaterial as a Benz enhanced my social value, along with my inability to access a modest $1,000, I was simultaneously enthusiastic about breaking my impoverished perception and immediately changing my financial paradigm!

As you read this, this is exactly what I seek to do in you: change your financial paradigm. Whether you are black, white, brown, purple or green, people of all ethnicities need to learn how to get a better grip on financial stewardship! I later learned that this inability to access $1,000 wasn't just a plight that the average African-American person faces, but it's true of the average American citizen altogether! According to a recent survey conducted by GoBankingRates in 2016, 69% of Americans have less than $1,000 in a personal savings account. This number was up from the same survey conducted in 2015 that suggested 62%. And what's even more noteworthy is that 44% of that 69% of people who couldn't get their hands on $1,000 of their own money made between $100k-$150k a year! 29% made more than $150k a year! Yet they still had less than $1k saved up in a savings account. So as you can see, managing money isn't a race problem; it's not even an income problem; it's a mentality problem!

Consumer Alert

The Industrial Revolution changed the face of American culture and marked a major turning point in history. This is the period in American history during which we swung from a primarily agriculturally driven economy to a largely industrial economy. Consequently, society changed from being groups of self-sufficient people to paycheck-dependent people. In other words, we became consumers.

A consumer, by raw definition, is a person who devours, uses up, feeds on, and even spends wastefully. And we became consumers because we were conditioned to be. In order for industries to be successful, they needed to train the rest of society to buy, use up, feed on, and spend wastefully on the products they produced. To do that, they marketed their products to society in such a way that people began to feel as if they needed those products to feel important, complete, and part of the elite crowd. Herein is where we as a people lost the sense of success and value in what we created, and misdirected it into the things we consumed. What we valued was no longer what we produced, but what we possessed. And over a hundred years later, much of our mainstream society is still living just as we have been conditioned to live—as consumers.

This is a consumer alert! An alert to wake you up to the fact that you have been trained to spend, buy, use, expend, and squander. And for many of you, this is all you know—spending! According to financial advisor John Cortinas, there are three money mindsets: 1) spend it; 2) save it; and 3) serve others with it. People who are financially sound are fairly balanced in all three areas; however, this represents a small minority of our society. Most people are unhealthy financially because they have absolutely no balance between the three options.

We have ample enticement and coercion to spend it, but who's teaching us to save it and serve others with it? How many commercials do you see on television a day encouraging you to save or serve people with a portion of your money? Who is helping you to be financially balanced? Who is encouraging you to gain financial freedom—that point in your life when you are no longer paycheck dependent, no longer stressed out or struggling trying to figure out what you're going to do if you miss your next paycheck or even fail to get a paycheck for the next nine months?

For the most part, many can answer that no one is helping them to establish balance between spending their money, saving it, and serving others with it. Consequently, just as a good conditioned consumer, all you do is spend, spend, spend. And for those who do somewhat save, because the industrial pressure to buy is so persuasive and formidable, in time they even manage to talk themselves into spending the little they have saved.

Hopefully, this work that I have put together will help you take heed to this alert and deliver you from being a full-blown consumer. It's time to break the industrial spell that has been placed on us for the last 100-plus years! It's time for us to *stop* consuming so much and start creating instead! We need to use our wealth, however much that is, to create financial freedom for ourselves and get ourselves to a place where we don't *have* to depend on a regular paycheck to thrive—or on the credit card industry to survive.

Credit Score

On his latest album **4:44**, Jay-Z asked the question during his track entitled, *Story of OJ Simpson, "You want to know what's more important than throwing money away at a strip club? Credit!"* Now we really didn't need Jay-Z to make most of us aware of this, but I appreciate him attempting to at least wake up the economic consciousness of his fan base with his music! The reality is that credit is important, and we need to do everything we can to understand it, as well as establish and/or maintain a healthy credit rating. Doing so positions you to do a range of business with the financial world, and to do it at an interest rate that is manageable. As a matter of fact, good credit is often the determining factor for many companies with lucrative job opportunities to extend an offer.

I could say a lot about America's credit rating system, but this is meant to be a rudimentary explanation. First, let me say that to establish or maintain good credit, you must have some form of debt. The credit system is designed to use the way an individual handles their debt as an analytical gauge to determine your financial character and your overall loan worthiness. Ideally, you want your credit rating to be north of 800. However, getting your score between 670-770 is socially acceptable being that the national average score is approximately 687. I call the 670-770 range the credit score sweet spot. A credit rating within this range is nationally smiled upon. Of course, if you can get it higher that's excellent. But generally, you can do good business with your credit rating in the sweet spot.

A few basic areas affect your credit score: *1) Payment history 2) Diverse debt (i.e. revolving, fixed/installment and open) 3) Length of credit history, and 4) Credit limit-High balance.* If you work on these four areas alone, it will certainly improve your credit score. Allow me to briefly explain each area, but I would encourage you to do further research as well.

1. Payment history: This basically refers to you paying your debts on time. If you are late making your monthly payment, it reports negatively and drops your credit score. The more you pay your debts on time each month, the more it improves your credit score.

2. Diverse debt: *Revolving debt* is any type of credit card (bank or store department). It is debt that revolves, meaning you are not required to pay the entire balance each month, but rather can make a minimum payment and revolve the remaining balance to the next month. The minimum payment can be different each month depending on your usage. *Fixed/ installment* debt include loans such as an automobile loan, home mortgage, student loan…etc. The monthly payment is fixed or is the same each month until the loan is paid in full. *Open debt* includes utility bills, cell phone bills, gas cards etc. The full balance for open accounts are expected at the end of each billing cycle. Though you can make a payment on these type of debts, if the balance is not paid in full in a timely manner, service for the account is usually interrupted until the full balance is satisfied.

21

3. Length of credit history: The age of your active debt works in your favor. The longer you have an account, the more it is helping your credit. This usually applies to credit cards and home loans. Auto loans generally last 5-6 years and are paid in full. However, home loans can remain on your credit for 25-30 years, and credit cards can remain even longer! People who don't understand this make the mistake of *trying* to fix their credit, and close all of their credit card accounts, or the ones with the highest balances, which immediately drops their credit score, because the cards they closed happened to be the ones they have had the longest! You *never* close old credit card accounts. A better option is to just cut them up or simply stop using them. But never close the accounts. You need old debt on your credit report to positively impact your score. Contrary, this is why you want to be careful applying for a number of new cards. Getting a new card will drop your score temporarily until you start making on time payments consistently for six-months to a year.

4. Credit Limit-High Balance: This applies mostly to credit cards. The credit scoring system (i.e. FICO) does not like you using your credit card too close to its maximum spending potential. If you have a card with a $1,000 limit, FICO doesn't like you charging too close to $1,000. Now the question is, "how close is too close?" The answer is 30%. If you use over 30% of your credit limit, FICO will decrease your credit score. This technically means that though you have a credit card with a $1,000 credit line, you really only have a $300 credit limit. So it is a good practice to distinguish between a credit *line* from a credit *limit*. A credit *line* is how much you can spend. A credit *limit* is how much you can spend before it starts hurting your credit. If you have a card with a $500 credit line, that same card has a $150 credit limit. Consequently, it is a good practice that if you can't pay your credit cards completely off each month, to at least try to keep them paid to their credit limit each month. This way, your credit card usage will not hurt your credit score, but rather improve it.

Again, if you are looking to improve your credit score, giving attention to these areas alone will noticeably improve it.

Swiper, No Swiping

When my oldest daughter Katelynn was a little girl, she owned a huge collection of cartoons and animated films that she loved so much she would watch them over and over again. I saw the movie *Pocahontas* so much I wanted to throw the VCR *and* the VHS tape out of the window! Thank God for "Blue's Clues" and "Teletubbies" because at least they gave us something else to watch. And then there came "Dora the Explorer." She loved Dora! This girl made me get Dora sheets, Dora curtains, Dora shoes, a Dora umbrella, and even a Dora backpack. Of all the characters in the show, the one I found most interesting is the character named Swiper; the little fox that would always steal from other people. He would literally swipe their stuff and run off with it. He had a bad habit of swiping! And every time Swiper would come around to steal somebody else's things, Dora and the gang would hinder him from robbing by simply saying three little words: **"SWIPER, NO SWIPING!"** They would repeat this again and again until they completely discouraged him from swiping.

How much more money would you have in your savings or checking account if every time you took out your debit/credit card to make an unnecessary purchase and get more stuff, you told yourself, "SWIPER, NO SWIPING"? What would your financial picture look like if you discouraged yourself from swiping?

Even though swiping is convenient, and considered a necessary evil, the con is that it doesn't allow you to see your money dwindle as readily as paying with cash does. When you swipe, you don't get the same emotional feeling that comes with a sudden financial depletion. You don't see the $20 bill broken, and all you get back is $5 and two dimes. All you do is swipe and go. It's just that simple. There's no immediate awareness of financial loss or account depletion—just the immediate satisfaction of a purchase, which triggers endorphins that give you that "feel-good" sensation. Swiping immediately puts you in a good mood.

But when we swipe without a budget in mind or any consideration of overspending, our swiping can become addictive. That's right! Many of us are addicted to swiping, and it's getting our homes in financial trouble. Consequently, we need to deter ourselves from so much swiping. Even though this is a swipe culture where swiping is a necessary evil, we still can't swipe so much that we overspend and rob ourselves of the financial freedom we should strive to enjoy. If you are over-swiping your debit/credit cards, then your swiping is robbing you of being free from paycheck dependence. If this is your ugly reality, learn to start denying yourself the temporary "feel-good" sensation by saying three easy words: "SWIPER (replace with your name) NO SWIPING!" "I have debts to pay—Swiper, no swiping!" "I want to retire comfortably— Swiper, no swiping!" "I need to pay off my student loans—Swiper, no swiping!" "I have yet to stash $1,000 in an emergency fund— Swiper, no swiping!" "I don't even have three months of living expenses saved up—Swiper, no swiping!" "I don't *need* more shoes, jewelry, gadgets, clothes, or latest products—Swiper, noooo swiping!"

Is This Fast for Me?

This fast is for you if you're financially frustrated. It's for you if you're at your wit's end about where to start to become more financially stable. It's for you if the stress of managing money is causing anxiety in your relationship with your spouse, friends, or family members. It's for you if you don't have at least three to six months of living expenses saved and tucked away in the event of sudden job loss or an unforeseen circumstance. If you make hundreds of dollars' worth of involuntary charitable contributions to your bank every year, and they send you a card or an e-mail notification thanking you for your "NSF" contribution to their bank, this fast is for you! This is for you if you aren't a consistent giver to the church through tithes and/or offerings because you feel you can't afford to tithe or give more than you do. If you normally have more days left in the month than dollars to manage on a regular basis, this fast is designed just for you. And if you just want to better discipline yourself financially to become a better steward over the finances that God has blessed you with, this fast is for you.

How does it work?

This fast is very simple. For the next few weeks, you will *only* spend money on bare essentials. Only meager necessities. But I have to be honest with you: even though this is a very simple idea, it's going to be a challenge to successfully put it into practice. Many of you are about to emotionally experience what it feels like to detox from a chronic addiction. However, you can do it!

During this financial fast, you cannot shop for any non-essentials or use any of your credit cards. For forty consecutive days, you must refrain from buying anything that is not a "real" necessity—no restaurants, no fast-food, no malls, no movies, no gift-buying, no hair salons (if you must, you can go, but no *outlandishly priced* styles; go basic if you *must* go—nothing beyond a basic trim, and style; no add-on services), no massages, no pedicures, no manicures, and no car washes/details (wash it yourself if you can). Stick with the bare essentials because this is about *contentment*! Also, remember that this *is* still a fast, so you must practice self-denial.

What can I buy?

I can't stress this enough—bare essentials. These include food, gas, bills, medicine, vitamins, personal hygiene supplies, toiletries, school supplies, cleaning supplies, etc. Let me add here that food doesn't mean cookies, chips, soda, candy, and so on. Those are snacks, which are really comfort/junk foods. Okay, if you *must*, go ahead, *but* don't overdo it. If you can just buy real food, that would be great. Instead of junk food, I would much rather you replace them with fruit or some other healthier snack.

Now, be smart and use your common sense on certain cases. During the fast, if you discover that your three-year-old's shoes have gotten too small, don't make the baby go for the next forty days with hurting feet. Go buy your baby a pair of shoes! Now if it's your teenager, that's a different story! They will survive! I'm joking. There will be items that come up that are indeed essential purchases. I advise you to employ your common sense. If your children are in a special event at school, pay the baby's fee. Don't make them suffer by not being able to participate in their special events. By the same token, however, all of their school events aren't "special."

So again, be wise. If you are planning to do this fast, use as much integrity as you possibly can. If it's essential, it's essential. If not, don't try to rationalize it into being essential. You can't cheat this fast. You can only cheat yourself.

What will I need?

A budget, a journal (or Word file), a copy of your credit report, a container to stash loose coins, prayer, and internal fortitude! This won't be painless.

What's expected of me during this fast?

During your time of financial fasting, you'll make many sacrifices. Here are a few ways you may increase your savings contributions for the next few weeks and get the most out of your sacrifices:

1. ***Eat as cheaply as possible***. Name-brand food items are *not* a must. Relax your expensive-brand taste buds for a while. Food-club and store-brand items taste pretty good. Also, buying more off-brand

items will cut your grocery bill noticeably. By cutting your grocery bills to the bare minimum, you'll be able to put more cash into your savings account or emergency fund. I'm talking about at least $100 or more in savings. It's not the end of the world—you can resume buying your normal name-brand items when this fast is over. But you may not want to after you see how much money goes back into your pocket! Also, try to make a meal out of the food you have without going shopping for the food you *want*. Exhaust your pantry items. Eat some meatless meals. Drink water. Open those canned goods way back in your pantry and season them up. Challenge yourself to completely clean out your fridge, freezer, and pantry before you go grocery shopping. You will be amazed at how much you can save by just doing this. I'm merely giving you a way to save *even* more than you already will.

2. ***Cut your entertainment expenditures down to nothing***. Forget going to the movies, concerts, or plays. Instead, take advantage of free ways to entertain yourself. Be creative. Do something that you have failed to do lately, like reading the Bible or other books. Go play in the park with your kids, take a walk with your spouse or a friend, play Internet games, chat with some of those friends you never talk to on your Facebook page, work out, or complete some of those household chores that you've been putting off. Get caught up on recent news events. Some of us have no clue about what's going on in the world. If you don't do something that intrigues and

fascinates you, these next few weeks won't be the most fun days of your life. So, you must be creative.

3. ***Don't buy any new clothes (or shoes).*** Clean your closet to discover forgotten clothes. Wear something you haven't worn in a long time (if it still fits). Mix and match clothes in your closet to keep your style fresh. Whether you clean out your closet or not, remember that during the fast you're not buying anything new.

4. ***Read the Word.*** Get the following scriptures into your spirit; Luke 12:15, Philippians 4:11-13, 1 Timothy 6:6-10, and Hebrews 13:5. Meditate on them until they truly begin to resonate with you. You can read other Scriptures as well, but these readings are the core readings to financial discipline.

5. ***Read your daily devotional and write in your financial journal.*** Let my 40 daily devotionals inspire and motivate you to allow this transformation to take place for you. Write down your personal reflections from my devotionals in your own personal journal, and indicate how they challenged or confirmed you. Record *everything* you spend daily. If you didn't spend anything, record that as well. Call your automated bank or go online and record your balance every morning and night. Write down how much your account increased or decreased for that day (e.g. -$33.17 or +$12.08). Remember, *every cent counts, so every cent should be accounted for*. Every single cent! Also, you can pray in your journal. Write down

your prayers and what you need from God as you experience this fast. Be sure to pray for contentment, financial wisdom, and protection from greed *daily*. Also, record how you are doing during the fast.

6. ***Never carry loose cash with you.*** You are not allowed to have any extra cash on you at any time if it is not for some "predetermined" essential purchase. Other than that, all of your money should be deposited into your checking or savings account. If you have to make a withdrawal from the bank, take out *only* what you need. If you use the ATM and are forced to take out too much, *as soon as possible, redeposit the extra money you did not need back into your account.*

7. ***Save loose change.*** Every *loose coin* you come across, save in a container. Coins on the ground at the gas station, under the dryer, in your cup holders of your car...etc Collect them all! Don't let your pride prevent you from picking up a penny! Remember, every cent counts! Save loose coins and deposit them at the end of this 40 day fast. Make it a habit in the future to deposit loose coins once a month into your savings. Even if it's nothing but $3.38 cents, *deposit it,* because *every cent counts.* If you don't have a savings account, open one as soon as possible. I recommend that you have at least two checking accounts and four savings accounts. Below is what I advise each account to be used for:

Checking account 1: *This is your business account.* The only money that comes out of this account is for your business transactions (rent/mortgage, bills, car note, insurances, groceries, gas for the car…etc).

Checking account 2: *This is your personal account.* You use this account for all of your personal spending. Only put enough in this account to cover your own personal spending (i.e. self-care, eating out, buying gifts, personal shopping, entertainment, etc.).

Savings account 1: *Emergency savings fund.* Place anywhere from $1,000 to $2,000 in this account and leave it alone until you have a real emergency (e.g. blown tire, non-working appliance, broken window, cracked windshield, unexpected emergency travel, or friendship/family loans). Always replenish what you use as soon as possible.

Savings account 2: *Personal savings.* This account is for vacations, getaways, big planned purchases (e.g. furniture, TV's, cars, down payment for a house, roof repair, etc.). Also, set up your accounts so that you can use your bank's mobile banking app to transfer money from one account to another. Most of your banking needs can be done now in the palm of your hands, which is very convenient. Check and see if your bank has mobile banking.

Savings account 3: *Long-term living expense.* This account is for you to *initially* accumulate six months of living expenses. Once you reach the six-month goal, increase the fund an additional month or two each year, and keep adding money to it until you need it (i.e. when your regular income temporarily stops coming in).

I believe the fastest way to create a six-month living expense account is not by depositing money into a regular bank savings account, but rather by utilizing a special mutual fund. You can have more than one mutual fund account just as you can have more than one checking or savings account with the bank. The wisest thing to do is allow your money to make money and grow for you as you make regular small deposits into it so that it will increase to the amount you want it to be. Once you reach that goal, why not just let it sit there and keep growing as you continue to make very small deposits into it? The good news is that if you never lose your job or regular form of income, and thus have no reason to tap into this account, your money can sit there and continue to grow until you retire. You can then draw from the account as an additional financial stream during retirement.

Savings account 4: The fourth type of savings account that you'll need as well is a retirement account. It works the same way as the third savings account. Do not put this money in a regular bank savings account. You need to open up a 401K or Roth IRA, or invest in some type of stock or mutual fund account to maximize your allowable deposits for a year so that you can start preparing for retirement. Again, you can have more than one stock account in your portfolio. I recommend that you research some firms to find the best one with whom to open this account if you don't already have a 401k or 403B or some fund designated as your retirement account. When you get it, maximize your contributions by putting as much money in it as you can. This is the account that you want to be most plentiful when you reach age 65 or whatever age you seek to retire. You want this account to have $1.3 million or more in it at retirement so that you can enjoy your last days on earth doing exactly what you want to do. This is not an account that you live off of *now*, but it's the one you plan to live off of *later,* once regular income stops coming in.

8. *Pay a debt off.* Pay off at least one debt during this fast. If you can retire more debt, go for it! It doesn't matter when you pay off the debts, but before this fast is over, pay off at least one debt of your choice. Again, if you can pay off more, that would be great. But at least eliminate one, no matter how small or large it is. If you can't eliminate the debt, pay as much on it as possible during the next forty days.

Now this really doesn't mean that $15 you owe your family member/friend. Even though that's a debt too, I'm talking about a debt that's affecting your credit and ability to do business in the business world. But now, if you owe your mother, Ashley from work, or Ray-Ray down the street, pay them the money you owe them as well!

9. ***Reduce utility bills.*** The idea of this fast is to save money and reduce cost wherever you can. One place you can easily reduce cost is through your utility usage. This month you can cut expenses like your water, power, and gas bills just by simply being more mindful of your usage. Turn lights off that don't need to be on. Stop sleeping with the TV on. Unplug appliances that you aren't using. Even though they're not on, you're still paying to have them plugged in. Stop heating/cooling your furniture for the eight hours you're at work. Cut your shower time from twenty minutes to five, or stop running a whirlpool's worth of water in your tub every night. Wash full loads of clothes. Cut your cable subscription back. Do you really need the platinum package with 2,000 channels when you only realistically watch 8-10 channels? Do you really need the latest fastest internet? I mean how fast do you need google.com to pop up on your screen? Did the last speed not bring it up fast enough for you? There is so much you can do to reduce your utility payments. Cut the cost, and then put the money you save into your savings.

10. ***Recoup and recover.*** Whether you realize it or not, money is laying around your home. Go on a scavenger hunt and look through every drawer, every item of clothing with pockets, behind the dryer and washing machine, in every purse, car cup holders, under the seats, beneath the couch cushions, under the couch, etc., and find

that valuable stuff called money that's just misplaced. In Luke 15 Jesus talks about a woman who lost one coin and swept her entire house until she found it. I assure you that you have more than one lost penny, nickel, dime, quarter, or dollar just aimlessly laying somewhere in your personal space. Find it and put it where it goes— your savings account!

Also, look around your house for items you've bought that still have tags on them or are still in the box that you can take back and get a refund. Look for things you can sell so you can make some money while on this fast. Don't just seek to conserve money for your savings while on this fast, but also think of ways to make money for your savings. Check your bills to make sure companies aren't charging you for services or "perks" you didn't sign up for. If so, stop them and recover that money. Cancel subscriptions that are eating away at your ability to save more. Check to make sure your rebates have come. Fill out your online surveys to get your free meals, gift cards, and whatever else they are offering nowadays. You get the idea. Recoup and recover!

11. ***Get a copy of your credit report and score.*** You can visit Annualcreditreport.com, freecreditreport.com, or freecreditscore.com to get a free credit report and score. You can also pay to get a report and score from all three credit reporting agencies. This would be considered a necessity, or you can do it in preparation for the 40-day fast. The government allows you a free

credit report once a year. So, if you haven't already pulled yours this year, get one. During this fast, meticulously check your credit report and make sure that *all* the information on there is correct and you are not being victimized by identity theft. Make sure you know who you owe and how much you owe them and that the balance is correct so you can get on the road to being debt free! You can dispute any account on your credit report, either online or by mail. Whatever account you dispute, they have a certain window of time to respond and verify that the information on the credit report is correct. If they don't, by law it has to be removed from your report. So again, analyze your report and work on it. I have seen people's credit score jump 10-30 points on this fast!

12. **Tithe!** Last but certainly not least, you need to honor God with the tithe on this fast. God said in Malachi 3:10, "*Put me to the test [by honoring me through tithing] and see if I won't open the windows of heaven and pour you out a blessing.*" Therefore, if you are presently not a tither, you need to begin honoring God with 10% of your earnings on this fast. Why? Because this fast is meant to align your financial stewardship with the will of God. It is God's will that we honor Him with the tithe out of a sense of gratitude for what He allows us to earn with the intellect, body functions, and talents that He has given us. We are to revere God with our resources, not replace Him or even rob Him with our resources. If you want what you do with your wealth to be blessed, don't sabotage yourself by robbing God of the honor due Him. If you never tithe

again, at least practice tithing during this fast. You may want to come back and do this fast again some other time, and when you do, tithe along with it.

Now, if you don't attend a church, first I advise you to find you a local congregation where you can worship and spiritually grow. Until then, you can send or give your tithe through any church as an act of honoring God. You can even visit many church's websites and give online. God doesn't care which church you choose to honor Him with your tithe. Just make sure to honor Him with it.

Finally, for all of the non-religious people who decided to read this book for strictly financial reasons, I pray that you find God and eventually open your heart to His Son Jesus Christ, allowing His Word to transform you. But until then, even though you don't believe in God or His church, understand that it's still considered a good financial practice to use a percentage of your money to be a part of something much bigger than yourself and serve others with it. I would advise you to find a charity that is special to you, and become a regular 10% donor. Or you can find several charities or non-profits and rotate your 10% contribution among them.

Whatever you do, don't keep all 100% of your income to and for yourself. Earmark 10% of what you earn to make a real impact in the lives of others through an organization or cause bigger than yourself. Even if you don't believe in God or believe in "church," many churches have food pantries that feed the hungry, community-based programs that house the homeless, help recovering drug addicts, serve children with incarcerated parents, and so many other things for which you don't have to be a believer in God or the church to donate. You just have to be a believer in what they are doing for others.

Ready? Set? Go!

That's it! You now have all you need to successfully complete this fast. I guarantee you that if you stick to the plan I have provided you by doing exactly what I have laid out for you, this fast is going to bless you every single time you do it. Buckle your seatbelts, because you're about to learn some things about yourself and your financial habits that you've never observed long enough to know they existed. You're about to see if you're controlling your finances or if your finances are really controlling you. But remember, this fast will only be effective if you allow yourself to "painfully" learn the lessons it is designed to teach you about yourself, and what it takes to be financially free. Are you ready? Set? *Let's go!*

Questions & Answers

What if my birthday or my spouse/child's birthday falls within the time of this fast?

Happy Birthday! Listen, people living in poverty celebrate their birthdays every day in this world. You don't have to spend money to celebrate a birthday or anniversary. Be creative! Cook dinner using the food you already have, or plan ahead and add those special ingredients to your grocery list and/or buy those concert tickets prior to going on this fast. But once you commit to this fast, you should be operating in the spirit of contentment— birthday/anniversary or not.

I have a cash back rewards credit card which earns me 1-2% cash back on what I spend. Should I stop using it while on this fast?

Great question! If you are earning money by using your card, I would advise you to continue using it, but wisely. *This means using it* only *for your basic needs like paying bills, grocery shopping, gas for your car, etc. But <u>as soon as you use the card,</u> pay it off <u>within 24 hours.</u> That way, you earn your 1-2% without accumulating debt. It basically becomes a debit card with cash-back rewards, and not solely a credit card anymore. But don't spend what you don't already have budgeted to spend, and you must pay back what you spend within 24 hours. That way, you are making the system work for you, not against you.*

What if someone asks to borrow money from me?

Repeat after me: "No." *How did that feel? This is an empowering word you need to learn to employ more often. You must learn the art (as well as skill) of saying* no *many different yet comprehensible ways, such as, "I wish I could, but unfortunately I don't have it"; "I'm not in the position to loan out money right now"; "At the moment, my funds are tied up." And my favorite response for repeat offenders:* "No problem! *I got you . . . as soon as you pay me back the money I let you borrow last time!" Now, if someone needs to borrow funds for a* dire need, *use your wisdom. Is this the first time you have ever loaned money to this person? If so, what is your maximum amount for a first-time loan? You'd better set one. This is a financial business matter, and you need to start handling your* financial business. *Whatever you loan out,* make sure *you either establish a repayment date for the full amount or a satisfactory payment arrangement. At this point, you need to become like a creditor: call, e-mail, stop by, or do anything else to get your money back. And if they default on your loan, that's somebody you never have to worry about loaning to ever again.*

I have tickets to a show during the fast. Can I still go?

Yes! You just can't spend money on anything while you're there. Also, find either free parking or the least expensive parking option. In some cases, it may be more profitable to catch a ride with Uber. Check into it. Or just park somewhere for free and enjoy the walk.

During this fast, would it be wise to cancel subscriptions that I don't need?

Yes! This would be a great time to cancel anything your money is going toward that you don't necessarily need, including magazine subscriptions, premium channel apps, cable (there are so many other ways to watch TV nowadays), etc. This would be a great time to suspend those subscriptions and put that money back into your own pocket.

What if my smallest debt is more than I can manage to pay off in 40 days even with this fast?

I would advise you to make an effort to pay on it as much as you possibly can during this fast. At least you can put a bigger dent in it than you would have before this fast.

I see I need to pay off at least one of my debts. What about the others?

Again, if you can pay off more than one, do so! If not, you'll still want to organize all of the debts you have. For old debt, call and find out your balance. See if you can negotiate a new repayment agreement or a payoff amount to settle the account. Maybe you can even negotiate a better interest rate or ask if they are willing to at least dismiss the interest that has accumulated over time. Also, before you call, see what the statute of limitations is in your state on debt collection. If the limitation is seven years, and your debt is six years and eight months old, you don't want to call or e-mail anyone *concerning that debt. Just wait four more months and let it fall off your record. Other than that, be someone your creditors can work with concerning any debt you have. Answer/return their calls, and work out doable deals and profitable arrangements.*

What should I do with all the money I save for the next 40 days?

You can do a combination of things: 1) Start a short-term emergency savings account. *I recommend that you open this account with at least $1,000. Most unexpected emergencies can be taken care of if you have access to at least $1,000 of your own money. 2) Start a six-month living expense account. Calculate how much you need to survive a month on* basic *needs for six months. This figure should include your rent/mortgage, car note, gas, food, basic utilities and such. Multiply it by six months. This is your living expense savings goal. Make regular deposits in it until you reach your six-month goal. Once you reach it, try to add another month or two to it a year until you reach a one-year amount. 3) Start an investment portfolio by investing in some stocks. 4) Pay off/on another debt. 5) Start a personal entertainment savings account. I recommend no more than $500. You can use this account to do some fun things that you want to do to stay balanced and enjoy life, such as going to the movies, taking an overnight trip, dining at a restaurant you've always wanted to try, attending a play or concert, getting a massage, etc.*

Can I buy cigarettes during this fast?

Technically, no. But if you have a smoking addiction, I realistically understand your perceived need to smoke. At least try to minimize your smoking to cut costs, which would be a win-win. That's more money you can save as you reduce your smoking habit. Also, try to quit by chewing gum or wearing a patch. But again, I understand the addiction component, whether it's cigarettes, alcohol, or soda. So, just do your best.

Am I able to give to charity of any sort on this fast?

Yes, you are well able to donate to charity or other special causes on this fast. It's called "sowing." If you are moved to sow financially into a movement, cause, person, or organization while on this fast, feel free to sow what you feel moved to sow. But just be led to do so—not forced into it by guilt. Let it be a matter of the heart.

Testimonies

I'm so thankful for this fast. Being aware is the key. I've been taking care of my mother's finances due to illness and didn't look at my automated deductions. Things I had not used in months. $118 woke me up real quick. I found a solid $600 each month to pay off my debt. It's a slow process, but God has been faithful.
~Wendy West

30 years old, single, In debt. Never been able to save any money. Max salary was around $63k. With this financial fast, I've been able to save about $5k in 40 days. I've paid off my car,. I've paid off a loan and all of my bills are caught up and in good standing. I became a consistent tither, and God blessed me with 3 new job opportunities! This fast has shown me that if I can practice discipline, take the time to plan my day, stop spending just because I can, and become content with all that God has already blessed me with, I can save money, pay bills, and truly enjoy life. This has been an amazing journey.
~Mallerie Baize

The Financial Fast was tremendously eye opening and brought a new awareness for me and my family especially concerning stewardship. Whereas I thought we did not have enough, the Lord showed me just how wasteful we had become with what He had provided. My thinking has been transformed when it comes to

money. It has been a life-changing journey and I look forward to what lies ahead.
~Cheryl Crosby

My husband and I told ourselves that this year we would start taking more meaningful steps to get our finances in order any means necessary. We went to a few classes, took some notes and it did help, but the discipline still wasn't there. We are a family of 8 so stuff comes up often. It's pretty hard to pay for those things when you don't have anything in your savings account. This was hard on the kids, but we all learned that we really didn't need the things we thought we did. Another thing we realized was we ate out, out of convenience. I thank God for this fast! Not only did it bring our savings from $0 to $2000 in 40 days, it brought the discipline that we needed to achieve our goals. We will continue to use this in our everyday life because it definitely made a huge impact!
~Diana Johnson

This fast was life changing. Unknown to many I was driving around on a suspended license for two months prior to the fast because "I didn't have any extra money" to pay this ticket. The ticket was only $249.00. After being committed to the fast, I was able to save a total of 1561.00 as well as pay my ticket off and reinstate my license. This fast changed my mindset and my entire life. I've never had a savings account over 150.00! Now I have $900.00 saved (I had to buy some tires). This fast has revealed to me where all of my money was going.

I was working two jobs when I really didn't need to. Now I'm down to one and have a little over $500 left monthly after I pay my bills and buy groceries. This is all because I became conscious of what I was spending!
~Eugene Wiggins

I did it and it was hard for me, but it made me take notice of such bad habits that I had; shopping and eating out and buying the kids any and everything they want! I was able to reduce my cable bill from $275 a month to $57 a month, and look at the savings ! Also I reduced our cell phone bill from $300 to $175. We were all renting phones for a monthly fee that was added into the bill but I paid those phones off and reduced the bill. Now no one can get a phone unless they can pay for it. Listen, I wasn't all in at first and to be honest, I actually slipped a couple times with all that I had going on, but I never gave in and it wasn't to the point of no return, but it definitely woke me up ! We ate out a lot previously and shopped a lot, but I now choose wisely and definitely think twice before eating out and shopping! We want to be financially fit!
~Dawn Boyer

I really didn't know what to expect coming into the fast. I knew that my finances were out of whack and I needed to get them in order, but as a single mom and a new divorcée, I was just too busy. When I took the first step, keeping track of my expenses, I couldn't believe that I spent over $380 on fast food monthly! And that was only for a

family of three (myself, my adolescence and my infant). It made me realize that I was living like we had a two person income, when I only had one income. I was using credit cards for lots of "wants" and living paycheck to paycheck. For 40 days we went without fast food, I opened a separate checking account for my bills, and I started stashing money in my savings. Even my kids jumped in to help. We went through old purses, coats, and dressers. We found over $94 in change and gift cards worth over $80. I was able to save $1100 AND, for once, I didn't overdraw my account by the end of the month. This fast has been a true blessing to me.
~Katrina Coleman

I would like to thank you for this financial fast. What I learned most was discipline. I was afraid to manage money before the fast. I didn't understand money & I didn't see how my money could grow. I always thought the solution was more money, but the solution is really more discipline. The fast forced me to embrace my habits daily. To consider if what I was doing in every facet of my life was working. For the first time I realized that consistency creates habits (good or bad) and the principle is not discriminatory. By mastering those small things and MANY more, my thoughts about money started to change. I saw how things get better and easier one day at a time.
~Precious Williams

Day 1
"Don't Be Stupid"

Welcome to day 1 of your financial fast! I am so excited that you are serious about changing your paradigm of how you manage your wealth, challenging yourself to become wiser financially, and becoming financially free. For the next 40 days, I will be sharing many tidbits from a biblical standpoint that will open your eyes and stimulate your mind concerning many aspects of wealth that I believe will help you in your quest to become free financially. Because I am a pastor, for the next 40 days, I will be drawing my talking points from a variety of places in the Bible. But don't worry, this journal is not meant to evangelize you if you are not a Christian or non-believer. Nor will this be a Bible study. I will simply be using different Scriptures to open many doors to various financial talking points that I believe will help you on your quest to find financial freedom.

To start, let's consider Proverbs 12, where it reads, "Whoever loves discipline loves knowledge, but he who hates reproof is stupid," and "The way of a fool is right in his own eyes, but a wise man listens to advice." These are two biblical proverbs from Proverbs 12 that we need to consider when challenging ourselves to improve the way we handle our money. Perhaps like myself, many of you reading this book didn't learn effective or efficient methods to manage your wealth; therefore, you need reproof, which also means correction.

The only way to truly correct your method of wealth management involves gaining exposure to information and listening to the advice of people who know what they are talking about.

I have dedicated this book to serve as a harvest of financial fruit that you can glean from. The plentiful sound financial advice I have provided here is intentionally basic, but at the same time insightful, revelatory, and effective if you would only heed it, allowing it to correct some of your financial habits and detox some of your money management routines that don't involve management at all, but rather mismanagement at best. In the words of Proverbs 12:1 and verse 15, don't be stupid! Let this book correct your toxic tendencies with money. Your method of handling money may not be as wise as you think it is. Listen to all the advice in this book, as well as in other places, that is ripe and ready to be harvested. Get the knowledge it offers for your growth, and you will prove to be a wise person instead of a fool with your finances.

Day 2

"Remember God"

It is important that we start this financial fast off right! In saying that, we need to begin by looking at becoming great stewards from a faith perspective. In other words, to be financially free, we must first learn to honor God with our money. Deuteronomy 8:18 teaches us that we should remember the Lord God because He gives us the power to get wealth. In other words, God enables us to earn income.

Whether you are a realtor, a teacher, a person who works at the shipyard, a mail carrier, a Fed Ex driver, an accountant, a coach, or a bank teller, God enables you with the physical and intellectual capacity to earn money. Even if you are currently drawing a retirement pension, it was God who enabled and sustained you to work those many years to receive those retirement dollars. He gives you the power (i.e. the ability, capacity, functionality, and competence) to get wealth!

Because He gives us the physical ability and the intellectual capacity to get wealth, according to the Bible, we should remember Him. We do that by honoring Him with a portion of what we has enabled us to earn. Proverbs 3:9-10 says, "Honor the LORD with your substance and with the first fruits of all your produce; then your barns will be filled with plenty, and your vats will be bursting with wine." In the 21st century, this simply means that when we honor God by giving

Him the first part of our income, which is what we call the tithe (10% of our earnings), God will favor us with plenty. Now, plenty doesn't mean millions of dollars. Of course, it could, but that's not what these verses promise. It simply means you will have plenty of money to satisfy your lifestyle so you will have enough for your needs and some of your wants. So we need to trust the Scriptures as we seek to better manage our wealth to achieve our goal of financial freedom. We need to start 'remembering God' by honoring Him through tithing for enabling us to earn whatever income we are fortunate enough to earn.

Day 3

"Contentment"

When doing this fast, most of you will discover just how much you have neglected the spiritual discipline of "contentment." Remember, this fast is geared to teach you many things about your financial habits, as well your ability to prosper if you stop being such a consumer. But it's also designed to be a spiritual guide to direct you towards "contentment." Contentment is the state of being happy/satisfied with what you have. Yes, that's a Christian discipline—being happy with *what you have* and not stressing about the stuff you don't have.

People love quoting Philippians 4:13, which says, "I can do all things through Christ who strengthens me!" But they never say anything about the previous verse. You'll miss the true meaning of verse 13 without verse 12. There, Paul highlights *contentment*—the state of being happy/satisfied and at ease. Verse 12 says, "I know what it is to be in need, and I know what it is to have plenty. I have learned the secret of being content in any and every situation, whether well fed or hungry, whether living in plenty or in want." He's saying that as a believer, he knows how to be at ease on both extreme ends of life's spectrum; whether he's hungry and living in want, or well fed and living in plenty. The secret is your relationship with Christ. Paul declares, "I can do all things through Christ who gives me strength." In other words, having Jesus, no matter if you have everything or nothing at all, is the principal thing!

Throughout this fast, you must learn how to be at ease—to be satisfied with Christ and stop being so consumed with craving that cup of morning coffee, eating out, buying shoes, going to a concert, getting your nails done, etc. If you invest more time in your relationship with Christ by living in the kingdom way through studying His Word and praying, you will suddenly be at ease in a place of psychological contentment as a result of truly having Him and drawing strength from Him. People constantly consumed with buying "stuff" are those who don't draw enough from their relationship with Him. Just attending a Sunday service once a week isn't enough. Instead, you need to strive for a daily walk with Christ by praying and reading His Word. According to Paul, this is the secret of true contentment. And in the 21st century, such contentment will deliver us from our addiction of consuming, and help us find financial freedom!

Day 4

"Where are you?"

I recall leading a Bible study many years ago about the "first times" of the Bible. I was inspired to do so one Sunday while listening to a pastor I once sat under in Atlanta, Bishop Dreyfus Smith, the founder of Wings of Faith Ministries. During one of his sermon introductions, he was rattling off a bunch of "first-times" that had ever taken place post creation. I was so intrigued that I decided to study more of these "first-times." In doing so, I came across something that inspired me to write a whole sermon. The first question of the Bible happened to also be the first question God ever asked man, in Genesis 3:9: "Where are you?" At first this seemed largely strange to me that an all-knowing God would ask the question, "Where are you?" as if His all-knowingness wasn't really all-encompassing! But of course, this wasn't the case at all; God was simply being shrewd. He knew exactly where Adam was. He was just trying to get Adam to face the ugly truth and verbally locate himself in the heart of the disastrous consequences of his actions. Adam was prompted by God to admit that he was not in the place where He intended him to be, but rather in a place of shame. For this is the beginning of deliverance—when you can verbally admit that you have made some decisions that have left you in a shameful place that God never intended you to be.

I pose God's question to Adam now to you: Where are you? Face your ugly truth and locate yourself. Financially, where are you? Where have your financial decisions left you ashamed and full of regret? Are you shamefully in over your head in credit card debt? Are you in a place where you have worked for over 30 years with nothing to show for it? Are you making $90,000 or more a year, yet living from paycheck to paycheck? Are you trapped in bankruptcy? Are you struggling to stay afloat because you're living above your means? Are you at retirement age and without a 401K or an adequate savings account? Are you hiding behind poor credit? Locate yourself! This is where your deliverance begins. Where are you? Wherever it is, stop blaming others for you being there. This is all you! And like Adam, who ended up killing animals to make garments for Eve and himself, you can only be delivered from this shameful and embarrassing financial place when you learn how to start making some sacrifices! What are some of the sacrifices you need to make to recover from the terrible and shameful place your impulsive financial decisions landed you?

Day 5

"Digging out of Debt"

What depresses a large percentage of Americans most is debt. Many just can't get their financial lives together because they are in over their heads in debt—medical debt, student loan debt, credit card debt, personal debt, debt with friends, and/or debt with family members. Indeed, debt is consuming many people's time, mental peace, and happiness.

Ironically, however, the biggest mistake we make when it comes to debt, is not getting into it, because to a certain degree, you need to responsibly accumulate some debt to be seen financially trustworthy by the banking world. But the biggest mistake we make with debt is ignoring it and not actively trying to settle it. We ignore phone calls, let payments go past the due date, refuse to call our creditors to make payment arrangements, and let our mailboxes run over with mail because we're afraid to receive a bill from a creditor.

Yet this is not the way to handle your debt if you want to be financially free. Romans 13:8 says, "Let no debt remain outstanding, except the continuing debt to love one another." The Bible instructs us to pay our debts. It is simply not a good witness for the faith when God's people don't honor their word to pay what they owe. It's like eating at a restaurant and walking out without paying the check. And we are financially irresponsible when we get into debt we can't manage, and/or fail to actively pay off our debts as soon as possible. So, call your creditors and make arrangements, or pay at least the minimum or whatever you can just to let them know you're trying to be responsible.

Now, don't get frustrated. You won't eliminate your debt overnight because it's a process. Debt is just like a business contract or weight gain: it's easy to get in, or put on, but it's hard to get out of and eliminate. *But just trust the process.* Keep chipping away at it, one payment at a time. Cut down unnecessary spending, and put that money you keep giving Chick-fil-A, eBay, and Amazon into the payment of your debt instead. I know you hate paying off debt, but if you really hate it that badly, *stop digging yourself deeper into it* and start digging yourself *out of it*! Let no debt remain outstanding, because it's the right thing to do. Pay your debts.

Day 6

"Some Things Money Can't Buy"

In Acts 8 Peter and John were laying hands on believers so that they might receive the Holy Spirit. One man named Simon the Sorcerer observed how the gift of the Holy Spirit was given to others just by the laying on of Peter's hands. Simon offered to pay Peter a significant amount of money for this ability to lay hands on people like he saw him doing. But in verse 20 (NIV), Peter responded, "May your money perish with you, because you thought you could buy the gift of God with money!" In other words, Peter frankly told Simon that his money couldn't buy the power of the Holy Ghost.

Something else that's powerful is the fact that not only can money not buy the Holy Spirit, money also can't buy happiness. This is something we need to realize. We spend so much time trying to be happy by purchasing a multitude of things, thinking the more we have, the happier we will be. But that happy feeling only lasts a fleeting moment. Before you know it, you're spending your money to chase happiness again. How much money do you need to waste until you realize that it won't buy you happiness?

Some people actually have exactly what you wish you had, and they're just as miserable as they can be. They *have* the mansion, the Maybach, the Louis Vuitton, and the diamonds. Yet with all they have, they still haven't managed to purchase happiness. If they could, they would have bought it by now! But happiness can't be purchased! So, stop burning through your money trying to make a transaction that will bring you happiness. Happiness is a state of mind, and there's not a monetary transaction available in the world that can help you to possess it. Instead, happiness must be unleashed. You have to choose to be happy. Find things that naturally make you happy and don't require money. Stop going broke or burying yourself in debt seeking happiness. Happiness is within you! Find it and release it!

Day 7
"Easy Come, Easy Go"

I can't stand it when people always try to introduce me to a get-rich quick scheme. I don't know why, but it bothers me to the core when people want me to become a part of their pyramid scheme: "If you get ten other people under you, and if they all get five people under them, and then those five get at least three people under them. . . ." Blah, blah, blah, blah! I almost cringe with anger when people who haven't talked to me in *years* suddenly pop up on my Facebook messenger with a fake message, "Hey, how you've been doing? I keep up with you on Facebook (even though they have commented or liked *nothing* I've posted). Have you ever heard of this special tea by this company called . . .?"

To this day, I haven't known *one* of my friends or associates who do this type of stuff and prosper. I'm talking prolonged prosperity. Instead, every two or three years they change to a new business or different product, but with the same old pyramid (sometimes with a twist here and there), with a new video passed down to them to show people like me about those who have done it and been successful to make it more believable and achievable for me. I have just about seen it all and heard every sales pitch, from Melaleuca to Amway to Herbalife. Everything is designed to recruit you and persuade you to recruit others so you can "make a lot of fast money"!

The reality, however, is that these get-rich schemes don't really work for the average person. And for those who are successful, they only work temporarily. When the prosperity starts to fade, they're off working on the next pyramid scheme, trying to bring over all of their friends from the last pyramid scheme for which they aggressively recruited them.

A shocking statistic reveals that 70% of lottery winners end up broke in less than five years. Seventy percent! That's almost everybody! Why is this such a norm? Proverbs 13:11 (NRSV) says, "Wealth hastily gotten will dwindle, but those who gather little by little will increase it." The Message Bible puts it this way: "Easy come, easy go; but steady diligence pays off." That's how you grow towards financial freedom: *little by little*, with this attribute called diligence! You don't need a get-rich quick scheme or a fast-money approach to be financially free. If you get money fast, you'll just lose it even faster, in most cases.

So take your time to accumulate wealth. Little by little, get your emergency savings where you want it. Using diligence, fund that six- to nine-month living expense account. Reduce your debt a little bit at a time, and increase your wealth with a steady, sound, disciplined financial approach. This way, you will appreciate the process and value your hard-earned money a little more. Get over the fast-money approach. Instead, save your money little by little, and gradually grow your wealth.

Day 8

"The Work of Your Hands"

God blesses our obedience and rewards our faithfulness to Him in many ways. One of the ways He rewards us is by blessing the work that we do. Deuteronomy 28 reveals how God desires to favor us when we live a life of obedience to Him. Verse 12 says, "He will send rain in season from his rich storehouse in the sky and bless all your work, so that you will lend to many nations, but you will not have to borrow from any." God knows it's a blessing for us to be debt free and financially free. And His Word says that He will bless us if we just obey Him and live a life that honors Him. But there are still some things that we must do first.

1) We have to put in that work! The Bible has *nothing* positive to say about people who aren't working on something. The Bible is very anti-lazy. For the most part, God isn't just going to do everything for us. We have to work! And when we work, God will bless what we're working on for us to gain financially. Job lost all he had at one point, but towards the end of that book, the Bible says God gave him double what he had lost. Now, I don't believe God just "gave" Job twice as much. I believe Job worked, and God blessed his work.

2) When God blesses our work, we have to also manage the finances our work produces. We should manage it in such a way that we can *lend* to others, and not waste it to the point that we have to *borrow* as if God never blessed us enough to be financially free. God blesses our work *so that* we can be financially free. He blesses our work so we can live independently from credit cards, unnecessary loans, and other debt. If you live a life that honors God, and God is blessing your work, don't mismanage what He has blessed you to have. Utilize it so that you can be a lender and *not* a borrower. Then you'll experience financial freedom, and free yourself from financial bondage.

Day 9

"Keep an Open Heart"

When asked what the purpose of money is, one person responded that it is to 1) spend; 2) save; and 3) serve others with. We don't have *any* problems with spending it; on average, we don't do the greatest with saving it; and for the most part, someone has to twist our arm or guilt us into serving others with it. We are so addicted to spending our money out of habit, and even out of greed to satisfy our own personal need to possess, that using it to serve others is usually the very last thing we want to do with our money. However, serving others with a portion of the money we are blessed to earn is important. Even though every respected religion, from Christianity to Buddhism to Islam to Unitarian to Hinduism, don't agree on everything doctrinally, they all agree on the importance of serving others and having compassion on the less fortunate.

First John 3:17 says, "Rich people who see a brother or sister in need, yet close their hearts against them, cannot claim that they love God." As Christians, we are admonished not to close our hearts to the poor because we would rather spend our money on ourselves. We are taught over and over in the Bible to use our finances to help others, which is a direct reflection of our love for God. This is one reason we should pursue financial freedom—so that we can contribute to causes bigger than ourselves. We can donate to cancer research; organizations that help the less fortunate, families that need assistance burying their dead, and hungry children; ministries that serve the community; and so many other causes.

Yes, money is to be spent and saved, but we should also use it as a tool to serve and help others. Don't pursue financial freedom *just* for your own benefit, but also so that you can contribute to causes that make a significant impact on the lives of others less fortunate than yourself.

Day 10

"The Left-out and Looked Over"

Ever since I was a teen, I have been fond of helping the poor. I can recall very vividly one summer day when I was in downtown Mobile, Alabama, in Bienville Square shopping in some of the downtown stores. I couldn't have been more than 17 years old, because I had just recently started driving. A homeless man suddenly approached me, which had happened to me many times before, but this encounter was different. This brother came up to me not caring to receive any spare change or food, but rather he was just hoping to get some socks for his feet. I looked down at his feet, and sure enough, he was barefoot. And being barefoot in Mobile, Alabama, during the summer isn't the best scenario. He explained to me that he had been robbed by other homeless guys the night before. They took all of his stuff, including the shoes that he had on his feet.

Immediately, my heart went out to him. I decided that I could do better than give him some socks. With so many sneakers at home in my closet, I could actually give him shoes! I rushed home and grabbed several pairs of socks, and then looked in my closet to see what pair of shoes I would give him. My heart was immediately convicted when I reached for the most raggedy pair I had. I said to myself, *Why would you give him your worst, when you have enough to give him your best?* Right then, I decided to give him my brand-new pair of Jordan's that I had only worn maybe three or four times.

When I returned downtown with the socks and shoes, he was shocked and started crying. I asked why was he crying. He said that people always tell him they will be right back but they never return, and yet I actually came back! Needless to say, the brother was happy about my generosity towards him. But let's look at his experience with other people. How sad that people who are blessed find it so unimportant to take the time to be a blessing to the poor. As people on the other side of poverty, we must do better.

Just as I realized back then even as a young teen while looking in my closet for shoes to give to a homeless man, we need to think about how many jackets, shoes, and shirts we can afford to pour into the needs of others. We must learn to use our wealth to help the poor, those whom my former professor calls the left-out and looked-over. God encourages us to help the poor in Deuteronomy 15:7-8. From this text, we learn that helping the poor is a responsibility that we receive from God because He has blessed us with so much. This passage says, "If there is among you a poor man, one of your brethren, in any of your town . . . you shall not harden your heart or shut your hand against your poor brother, but you shall open your hand to him, and lend him sufficient for his need, whatever it may be." That is clear enough all by itself. When God blesses you to be in a good place, whereby you have enough both for your needs and to share with others, you should be willing to open your heart and hands to help the poor.

Giving is what makes a human being human, and balances the universe of all the ill things that transpire among us as people. It is all in our compassionate gestures of sharing what we have with someone else who doesn't have anything at all. So, as you continue to work on becoming more responsible with your finances, consider the responsibility that you must contribute to the needs of the poor instead of being so tight-fisted and hard-hearted. For part of the responsibility of being wealthy is the willingness to give some of it away.

Day 11

"Stop Being Prodigal"

In Luke 15, Jesus tells a string of parables to emphasize His personal obligation to seek out the lost. In the final and longest parable, he talks about a prodigal son who received a significant portion of wealth from his father (his due portion of his father's inheritance), by which he was expected to go out and make a fruitful life for himself. However, the parable says that the son instead went out and squandered all the wealth his father had given him, so he ended up broke. As a matter of fact, this is what "prodigal" means—to waste resources or spend money recklessly. According to the parable, the son wasted the wealth provided to him by his father on self-gratifying pleasures. Allegedly, he spent his money on prostitutes. Thus, he ended up trying to survive in a less than ideal situation, living way below the potential his financial situation once afforded him, and trying to make the best out of a mess. He lived his daily life as if his father had never provided him with the necessary wealth to build a self-sufficient sustenance.

What about you? Is the place your life is positioned today a reflection of the wealth God has blessed you to have? I'm not talking about millions and billions of dollars at a time. It could simply be that $48,000 annual salary you have, or once had. Is your life a reflection of the $73,000 you've made every year for the last six years? Or are you more like the prodigal son in Luke 15? Even though you have been fortunate enough to have wealth come into your hands, you squandered it by entertaining yourself and fulfilling your own personal pleasures, such as shopping, eating out, taking exotic vacations, and upgrading to the fastest and most recent technology. Proverbs 21:17 says, "People who love pleasure become poor; whoever loves wine and oil will never be rich."

Work on being wiser with your wealth. You can't just spend your money on personal pleasures constantly and expect to be financially free. Instead, be a good steward of the wealth your Father has allowed you to amass by making sound decisions with it. Stop being prodigal!

Day 12

"Act Your Wage"

At one point in time, Adam and Eve had it all. Because God had given them dominion and authority over the entire earth, everything was theirs. God even set them up with the most luxurious housing accommodations by placing them in the Garden of Eden, where they wanted for nothing. However, even though they had it all, they still pursued what was outside their range of possession. God had placed one tree out of their range, and commanded them not to pursue it. Yet, due to greed, they crossed the line anyway, and went well pass their range, and it cost them everything they had. Life became very uncomfortable for them for the rest of their lives, all because they went after stuff that wasn't in their range.

What have you lost, and what pain and discomfort have you brought upon yourself because you keep doing things outside of your financial range? Perhaps you do things you can't afford to do, buy things you can't afford to have, or spend your last dollars on things just to be able to say you had it or did it. I often tell people, "You need to learn how to act your wage!" In other words, "Stop trying to live like a six-figure salary earner when all you make is lower middle-class money." The same applies to anyone, no matter how much you make. If you make $33,000 a year, you shouldn't be trying to do everything that people who make $71,000 a year do.

Your wages won't be enough to cover the costs. Your money isn't long enough.

When you learn how to act your wage, you understand when you need to order from the appetizer side of the menu while everybody else is making selections from the entrée side. As a matter of fact, acting your wage gives you the wisdom to know that with the money you make in addition to the expenses you have, you have *no business* dining at a restaurant where they simply put numbers without dollars signs next to the food choices—or where they don't list the price at all.

Act your wage and stop venturing outside of your financial range for things. All you're doing is exhausting the little wealth you have and inviting needless discomfort into your life. Stay within your financial range, and learn to enjoy the things at the level you can afford them. You can't live a yacht life with paddle boat money! I'm not saying you can't buy a ticket to that concert, but stay in your own price range. Don't spend half of your paycheck to get floor seats. Get the $15 tickets and enjoy the show. Trust me, you won't be the *only* people sitting in the rafters. In everything that you do, stay within your range!

Day 13

"Keeping Up with The Joneses"

Yesterday we discussed how Adam and Eve invited pointless discomfort into their lives and lost what they had because they ventured outside of their range to consume the fruit produced from a certain tree they were instructed not to touch. They became a consumer of a product that was way out of their range. But if Adam and Even knew this fruit was not within their reach of consumption, why did they choose to go after it and become a consumer of it? The answer is found in Genesis 3:5. Eve was bamboozled by a marketing strategy that's still victimizing millions of people today. The Bible says Eve was tempted by the serpent to eat the fruit because in doing so she would *"be like God."* Verse 6 says that she took the fruit and ate it, seeing that by possessing it and consuming it, it would help her to gain what God had (wisdom and knowledge). She ate the fruit and gave some to Adam. They had a preoccupation with being like God, and it drove them to go after something that was way out of their range.

We call this mentality today, "keeping up with the Joneses." People with this obsession try to be like somebody else in regard to living where they live, driving what they drive or something similar, wearing what they wear, frequenting places they frequent, joining clubs they join, and doing what they do. Even though they don't like to admit it, millions of people hurt themselves financially by trying to be like somebody else they can't be.

This obsession begins as a child. How many times did you beg your parents to buy something you didn't have, but other kids in class had it and you wanted to be like them? Parents are pressured to buy $200 sneakers for their children because they want to be like their peers and wear what they are wearing. This obsession hurt the very first humans on earth, and it's still victimizing us today. Some people spend their whole week's paycheck or half of their monthly income to go to the club and "pop bottles" because they want to be like P-Diddy, Floyd Mayweather, and other celebrity personalities they follow on social media. We need to stop victimizing ourselves by self-mutilating our own net worth trying to "be like" somebody else with a lot more financial clout than we have.

Be yourself and stay on your own financial level. Stop chasing after someone else's lifestyle when you don't have an income anywhere close to their financial ability. Live within *your* means, not within the means of *others*; because when you use your means to live within the means of others, it will only cause you to be above your means and land you in serious debt.

Day 14

"Stop Pretending; Start Pretending"

Proverbs 13:7 reads, "Some pretend to be rich but have nothing, while others pretend to be poor but have great riches." This is so very true! Usually the people trying to live in a flashy way are just as broke as they can be, and those who live modestly are actually very wealthy, if not at the least financially comfortable. I met a millionaire many years ago, and over time we became good friends. The whole time we shared a friendship together, I *never* would have imagined that he was as wealthy as he was. He was a very humble, modest-looking guy. He never came off as flashy because he didn't show off any extras such as expensive jewelry. As a matter of fact, the only jewelry he wore was an average-looking wedding band and perhaps a Citizen watch. I can't remember what kind of car he drove, but whatever it was, it wasn't luxurious. He was very common-looking to the eye. When I found out he was financially loaded, I was floored!

When I asked him about it, the abovementioned Scripture was the one he referenced. He said, "D.L., it's the people who show off like they have so much that have so little, and the people who are humble in appearance that have real wealth." He said in so many words, "I don't wear my wealth, place it into depreciating possessions, or put it on display for all to see. If you want to see my wealth, you will have to check my portfolio, my mutual funds, my bank accounts, and the property that I own. My wealth isn't on my wrist, on my feet, or parked outside in the parking lot."

I must admit, after that conversation I was still dumb as a mule! I felt so honored that I actually knew a millionaire instead of being blessed and empowered by the financial wisdom he had just dumped on me within a five-minute conversation! But the wisdom itself that he shared was biblically rooted. If we want to build true wealth, we need to stop being so consumed with impressing our peers and creating haters for ourselves by accumulating things for them to notice us and be jealous of us, but rather start living like we don't have much at all. When we do get much, we need to keep living like we don't have much. We still should keep shopping for deals, eating out on nights when the kids eat free or at places with "2-for-1" promos, buying at Wal-Mart, ordering offline, packing a lunch for work, getting the most use out of everything we have, thrifting, and practicing frugality. That's what people with wealth do.

You would think that the most frugal people in the world would be those who don't make much money at all. But it's essentially the people with money who are living out Proverbs 13:7, pretending like they don't have money when in fact, they do. We need to stop pretending in a way that's keeping us broke and start pretending in a way that will help us build wealth. Stop living like you got it, and start living like you don't have it! If you practice this long enough, you might actually acquire a good amount of wealth!

Day 15

"Temptation to Spend"

Fasting is hard to do, no matter what type of fast it is (no meat and bread, no social media, no sweets, no processed food, or no spending of money). Whatever fast you do, it will come with its own unique trials and temptations. Believe it or not, you will be tempted to *spend money* on this fast for shoes, fast food, a snicker bar, a gift, a drink, etc. And the temptation will be very real! When Jesus fasted for forty days and nights, he also was tempted again and again and again (Luke 4).

Why so much temptation? Whenever you are trying to order your life in a way that glorifies God and benefits you, the Enemy will fight against that. The Devil wants you to stay in financial bondage. He doesn't want you to be free—free to give to others, free to fund God's kingdom, free to live your life above reproach, free to live without greed and discontentment, free to live your life in joy and happiness, free to live apart from financial worry and anxiety, and free to thank God for your prosperity.

The Devil will also tempt you because he fears the impact you will have once you complete this fast. This fast will give you financial confidence and power. No, this fast alone won't make you rich. That's not what it's about. But it will help you develop basic constructive financial habits that will get you on the path towards building wealth for yourself and make you more comfortable handling your finances.

You will also become proficient enough to teach the next generation of your family and God's kingdom to start early in their quest to be financially free. Famed poet Maya Angelou once said, "When you learn, teach!" Since teaching involves empowering others, you will become a vessel of empowerment. And the Enemy doesn't want that for you, or for those within your sphere of influence. Therefore, he will tempt you so that you'll fail in this fast. But God and I want you to succeed. So resist the Devil and his temptations. Know why you are being tempted and keep the benefits of your budding financial freedom before you. Like Christ, use the Word to defeat the Devil's temptations to spend and waste your wealth, and overcome him. You can do it!

Day 16

"Chasing Wealth"

King Solomon was said to have been the wisest man to have ever walked the face of the earth, not including Jesus Christ. Solomon was also one of the wealthiest men of the Bible. Consequently, as the wisest and one of the wealthiest men of the earth, what was Solomon's sagacious and learned view concerning wealth? Solomon had plenty to say about wealth in Proverbs and Ecclesiastes (Scholars say Ecclesiastes contained his views of later life). First, he said that it was meaningless trying to work so much in order to amass wealth in an attempt to be happy. Speaking from experience, Solomon argues from his pessimistic point of view of having it all.

In chapters 2 and 5 of Ecclesiastes, Solomon conclusively presents to us that he was so wealthy there was nothing his eyes saw that he could not have. He says that every pleasure he could experience, every possession he could acquire, and the most beautiful women he desired were all his to enjoy.

Solomon wanted to determine to what extent one could find the key to life in a diverse use of great wealth. At the end of this experiment, he discovered that money, along with the pleasures it can buy, is not the key to life, nor does it lift us out of the realm of life's frustrations or make us exclusively happy. He found that the present enjoyment of what we have is our only reward, but then even that thrill fades away. Then we're off to the next thing to spend our money on to make us momentarily happy again, like drug addicts going for their next high. Other than that, Solomon says having an abundance of money is meaningless because even though we have it all, we still can't find real happiness through it—and though filthy rich, we still die.

Thus, Solomon presents the futility of chasing wealth in and of itself: *It does not satisfy.* We will never reach the point where we have enough money to make us exclusively happy. Therefore, we shouldn't let our lives become just about accumulating money. We shouldn't chase after money, thinking that having more of it is the key to our true bliss, because it's not. Money won't make us happy. As Solomon finally realized, real joy comes in gaining the wisdom of God, which involves knowing God, fearing Him, and living a life pleasing unto Him. To the wealthiest and wisest man in the world, this is the core of true bliss—having a relationship with God.

Day 17

"Slave to Money"

Having money is good, but money having you isn't! Many people think they have money, but actually, their money has them. In other words, they are in bondage to their wealth! Their financial enslavement is different from that of people who aren't rich and have a bunch of debt. In Matthew 19, Jesus is approached by a wealthy young man who wanted to know how to inherit eternal life. Jesus told him to simply live by the sacred Word of God. In response, the young man claimed to already be allowing God's Word to guide the way he lived his life, and now he wanted to know what more he could do. Jesus directed him to sell all of his possessions and then give the money to the poor (the homeless, orphans, widows, immigrants, and physically disabled). Jesus told him that by serving the poor with his wealth in addition to already living out God's Word, not only would he have eternal life, but he would also amass wealth in heaven. But the young man went away saddened because selling his things and giving money to the poor was too hard for him to do. He had placed himself in the chains of financial bondage. He thought he had wealth, but instead his wealth had him!

Now, Jesus was a little extreme in asking the man to sell all of his property and give the money to the poor. Yet the principle is the same for those of us who find it hard to give a fraction of our wealth in the name of serving others. When we can't release some of what we have to help another human being much less fortunate than we, it means that we're in financial bondage! Our wealth possesses us. It is our god and master.

God is not pleased with those who allow their money to put them in such bondage. In Matthew 19:24 Jesus even said that it was hard for rich people to enter the kingdom of heaven because they won't do kingdom things with their money, like giving it to the less fortunate! I implore you not to make it hard for yourself to enter into the kingdom. Instead, value the acquirement of wealth in heaven as much as you would value acquiring it here on earth. Just as you do the right worldly things to build wealth here in the world, do the right kingdom things to build wealth in heaven. Regardless of how much or how little money you make, reserve some portion of it to serve the less fortunate. By doing so, you will store wealth up for yourself in heaven.

Day 18

"The Power in Your Mite"

Yesterday we discussed using our money to serve others. We don't need to have great wealth to give to something that's bigger than ourselves. In Mark 12:41-44, we find a perfect example of this principle. It's important that we grasp this concept because we can't get trapped into believing that we must have a certain amount of money to be able to give. This faulty mindset says that if all you possess is a dollar, you might as well keep it in your pocket because giving nothing but a dollar doesn't impress God. Kingdom giving, however, isn't about "amount," but about "attitude." It's about the heart!

In this text, we find a poor widowed woman who gave less than any American coin we have. For some reason Jesus was watching who was giving and what they were placing in the temple treasury box, which is equivalent to what we call the church offering plate today. He observed this woman putting in two mites. A mite is simply the name of a certain valued coin, just as we have names for our coins (e.g. penny, nickel, dime, quarter). The two mites she gave didn't even equal the value of one of our pennies. As a matter of fact, it takes five mites just to make one American penny. Which means she put less than a penny in the church offering plate. Thus, what she gave to help the church minister to others was equivalent to just half a cent.

Now, if we were sitting where Jesus was and saw this, we would have looked at her and said, "Are you serious, lady?" But Jesus' response was this: "This poor widow has put in more than all those who are putting a lot of money into the box. For they all contributed out of their abundance, but she out of her poverty." Although she didn't have much, she still had a generous heart of giving. She still understood the importance of giving out of what you have to something bigger than yourself. Now, as of 2017 the poverty level in America for one person is $12,060 a year, or $231 a week. If this woman could give two mites out of her extreme poverty, surely we all can give something out of what is called poverty for us today. So, stop talking yourself out of giving. Whatever you make, you can give something. And this scripture has us to see that God will honor us even more when we give something out of our poverty—even if it's just a dollar, or no more than a penny!

Day 19

"Sitting at The Feet..."

One night I was lying in bed just thinking. At the time, I was in the middle of preaching a series at my church called, "Living In the Key of F: Financial Freedom," and my mind was just consumed with every financial concept there was to think of. While lying in bed, I decided to Google how to save $10,000 (At the time, my wife and I were on pace to save that exact amount during the first six months of the year because we wanted to pay our truck off). But I had never read an article giving advice about sound strategies for doing so. After looking at a few articles, I felt really good, because we were already doing 90% of the suggested methods. As a result, I asked myself, *Why limit myself? Why not Google articles on how to save a million?* So I did!

After looking over several articles, one consistent piece of advice that I kept seeing again and again was investing in securities like mutual funds and getting involved into real estate. Nearly every article I gleaned from contained all the suggestions mentioned for saving $10,000. However, the most noticeable difference in the advice given for making a million involved real estate and investing. It seems that nearly every person who has made millions of dollars was advised this way.

I cannot stress enough the importance of listening to the advice of others. It is vital that we seek out advisors and sit at their feet to glean the necessary insight we are hungry for. It reminds me of Luke 10:39-42. One sister named Martha was busy in the kitchen serving, while the other sister, Mary, was sitting at Jesus' feet, taking in every syllable that fell from His lips. When Martha complained to Jesus that her sister wasn't helping in the kitchen, Jesus responded to her that Mary had chosen to do something that would not be taken away from her. She chose to sit at His feet and be guided by His wealth of information so that she might apply it to her everyday life!

Whose feet are you sitting at? Who are your financial advisors? Who do you listen to so that you can take their guidance and apply it to your financial situation? And don't be narrow minded in thinking that these are people you must have personal access to or be able to readily touch. You can sit at another's feet by reading their books, attending their seminars, or subscribing to their YouTube channel or their podcast. Many of our problems come from the fact that we aren't sitting at anybody's feet. Instead, we're just winging it ourselves with no type of direction at all—just living from paycheck to paycheck, doing what we've always done with our money because we never took the time to sit down and let someone pour financial wisdom into us. But according to Proverbs 11:14, "Without guidance, an entire nation falls; but with guidance, that same nation finds victory." If you want to be victorious in your finances, sit at somebody's feet and let them pour into you. Read articles and subscribe to periodicals that will give you access to wealth-building information. Stop being busy with your own plans, and get in a position where you can glean the necessary insight that will help raise you to the next level in the way you manage your wealth.

Day 20

"Grind"

Yesterday I shared with you how I came across some insight concerning making a million dollars. Nearly all the articles I read advised that in order to make a million, one needs to start investing and getting into real estate. Real estate investments involve things like buying homes, putting $5,000 to $10,000 into them and then relisting them on the market to turn a significant profit. But doing something like this takes work. You can't be lazy and make a million, unless you have a rabbit's foot in one pocket, a wishbone in the other pocket, and your lucky pair of underwear on—along with the luck of the Irish on your side. Some people who were just as lazy as they could be had some, if not all of these things, and landed millions of dollars. But these wild cases were exceptions to the rules.

For the rest of us without lucky underwear, Irish luck, or a wishbone/rabbit's foot in our pockets, we must rely on established principles that are consistently found everywhere—in the secular world, the spiritual world, the business world, and such. Proverbs 10:4 tells us that hands that don't want to work make you poor, but hands that work hard bring wealth to you. In other words, people who are lazy will never come into wealth. People who work hard will undoubtedly achieve financial success. It's a tried and true principle.

Now of course, working hard and bringing in the wealth is not enough to possess financial success. Along with working hard and bringing in wealth, you must have a strategy to manage the money you're bringing in. Yet a strategy without your resolve to grind in order to attract wealth into your hands is all for nothing as well. You need them both! But it starts with you putting your hand to a plan.

You can't be lazy. You can't sleep in bed until 10:00 a.m. every day. You can't be allergic to reading. You can't play video games all weekend when you could be attending a class or some sort of forum organized to expose you to the insight you need. You have to get up, think, go, move, attend, connect, meet, network, etc. In other words, you have to grind! If you're not willing to work for this wealth, you will remain stuck in the same financial place you say you don't like to be in. But if you go after it day after day, you will attract financial success to yourself and have the resources to be financially free.

Day 21

"Get Your House In Order"

Death is such a morbid subject. None of us like to talk about dying because it makes us uncomfortable. But regardless of how we feel about death or dying, it's a part of life that we all must face one day. Because this is such a grim, unavoidable truth, we should be wise while we live, using the time we've been given to prepare for our death. We should put things in place so that those we leave behind can still benefit from the wise decisions we made financially while we lived, and so that things will not be unnecessarily chaotic after our departure.

This is the same advice given to King Hezekiah in 2 Kings 20 by the prophet Isaiah. God inspired Isaiah to tell the sick king that he was about to die, so he needed to use the time he had left to get some things in order. The prophet tells King Hezekiah, "Get your house in order, for you shall surely die." How detrimental would it be to your loved ones if you failed to ensure your family's financial welfare in the event of your death? You never know when your time to die will come. Death is usually an unexpected occurrence. Although we expect to die someday, we just don't know exactly when. Therefore, we need to wisely set some things in place, knowing that death will indeed come for us all.

Is your house in order? Will your family financially suffer or profit by your departure? Will they suffer the tragic loss of both you *and* your financial support? Or will they at least be able to say that you were wise enough to leave an inheritance for them? If your family will need to rely on a go-fund-me page to bury you, you need to get your house in order. If you don't have term or whole life insurance, buy it. Who are the beneficiaries of your retirement fund or mutual funds? Do you have a living will? Is anyone listed on your personal bank accounts to access your funds in the event of your death? A lot of things need to be considered in preparing for your departure from life, all of which are a must. So, make those decisions now that will ensure you have something to leave your family that will make living without you a little easier. Get your house in order!

Day 22

"Money Doesn't Grow in The Ground"

I wrote the basis for this 40-day financial fast back in 2011, before I married my beautiful wife in 2012. So, I decided to pull it out in 2017 for the first time during our marriage to see how well we would do together. And as expected, we did amazing! It was exciting to finally get my wife on the same wavelength with me when it comes to a healthy financial paradigm. One of the things that we did during the fast that I was proudest about was starting her very first Roth IRA account. We had been talking about building financial security for retirement, along with the primary way wealthy people actually build wealth—investing.

Regardless of how much money you make, you will never build true wealth *just* by working a job and pinching 10-20% of your paycheck to deposit into your savings account. Savings accounts are good places to put money for vacations, emergencies, gifts, personal spending, entertainment, weekend getaways, and so on. But they aren't good places to put your money in order to build wealth. Your money doesn't significantly grow in bank savings accounts—not paying you 0.03% interest, it won't.

If you are placing all of your money in a savings account with a bank, you are like the man in Matthew 25:18 who was given money (one talent) to invest; but instead he buried it in the ground, placing it where money doesn't grow. Yet the Bible says that the others who were given talents put their money in a place where it doubled! They invested their money, empowering it to grow in time. It wasn't overnight, but patient growth. Verse 19 says it was "after a long time." It took time, but the one who had five talents doubled them to ten. The one with two doubled his to four. Only the one who put his money in a place where money doesn't grow still had the exact same amount of money (one talent).

This is the difference between putting your money in a savings account with your bank versus an investment account. Let me help you see it with real numbers. Let's say you deposited $1,000 in a savings account that yields 0.03% a year, which is what one of my banks currently offers. If you just let it sit there and "grow," after five years you will have a whopping $1,001.50! That's right, you would have pretty much buried $1,000 in the dirt! Now take that same $1,000 and place it in an investment fund. Let's say it was a fund that has averaged a 9% annual return for the last five years, which is exactly what one of my funds has produced. After one year, you will have $1,090, which is more than the five-year amount with the bank already. However, in five years, you will have $1,538.61! In five years, your initial $1,000 investment will have earned you $538.61 sitting in an investment fund, in contrast to only $1.50 sitting in a savings account at a bank. So you see, money that you need to be growing for you shouldn't be buried in a bank's savings account. Bank saving accounts are only for money you plan on spending within the next few months to a year, and that you need to be on hand and readily accessible for specific purposes. So don't be like the one-talent man in Matthew 25:18. Stop burying all of your money in the dirt! Put your money where it will grow—somewhere it has a better chance to double or maybe even triple after a long time. Invest your money and let it grow for you!

Day 23

"Turn Down"

I love NBA basketball. Recently, the National Basketball Association has been using hip-hop rapper Lil Jon as their musical promoter of NBA primetime games. For the commercials, they used the music from one of Lil Jon's hit singles, "Turn Down for What?" It's a rap song that's about partying all night long and never letting the party end. The question, "Turn down for what?" is essentially asking what possible reason is there to stop partying? The implication is that there is absolutely no reason! It suggests that when the party gets going, we should stay turned all the way up and keep partying for as long as we can. But when the NBA signed Lil Jon on to promote their primetime games, he decided to remix the song and insert an answer to his question, "Turn down for what?" In his song, he found that the one valid reason to turn down and stop the party was to watch NBA in primetime and see some of its greatest stars like LeBron James, Stephen Curry, James Harden, and Russell Westbrook battle it out on the court.

There are also some financial reasons why some of us may need to consider "turning down." The main reason is simply because we can't afford to stay turned up! Living a party life is expensive! Going out every weekend, buying expensive drinks, sitting in the VIP section, attending nearly every social outing, buying new outfits, eating at expensive eateries for social meetings, and just going, going all the time can be financially taxing. Now, the pictures/videos of you doing these things all the time look good on your Instagram, Snapchat, Facebook, and Twitter pages, but if you took a picture of your checking account after every event you were turned up at, and posted it, it wouldn't look as good. As a matter of fact, it would suggest that you really need to stop being turned up so much and turn down!

Jesus asked the question in Luke 14:28, "Which of you, desiring to build a tower, does not first sit down and count the cost, whether he has enough to complete it?" This is wisdom. Like those desiring to build, we need to learn how to look at our finances and figure out if we can truly afford to be as turned up as we are trying to be, or if we need to turn down. We need to learn how to count the cost. And when counting the cost, we need to be honest with ourselves about whether we have enough to do what we desire to do.

You will find that your account will often communicate to you that you need to pass on some of the things you desire to do because it costs too much and you just can't afford it. Learn to count the cost for everything you desire to spend your money on. If you don't have enough to do it, *don't!* Stop spending your money on things you can't afford to spend it on, and learn how to turn down.

Day 24

"New Wine Skin"

Late last night I was reading Luke 16 and ran into a real simple but thought-provoking truth in verse 10: "Whoever can be trusted with very little can also be trusted with much, and whoever is dishonest with very little will also be dishonest with much."

Let me ask you a question: Why do you keep asking God for more money, higher-paying jobs, promotions, and other income streams when you are reckless with the little money you do make? If you can't budget your $721 weekly paycheck, getting a promotion to make $1,021 weekly won't change your financial problems or change you. The *same* practices you use to manage that $721 check will be managing that $1,021 check as well. Winning the lottery isn't the solution either because the same mindset that controlled your money before you played the lottery will still be in control after you hit it. That's why your number never comes up!

You will just be making more expensive emotional purchases and still end up broke, and what you have will go to waste. Jesus once taught that you can't pour new wine in an old wine skin and expect to keep it. The fermentation of the wine will swell the old wine skin and cause it to break, spilling all the wine. Financially speaking, you can't put new money in the same old financial mindset and expect to retain it. Your new money, however much it is will end up wasted. To resolve this situation, you need a new financial paradigm. You need to adopt new concepts about your money, along with new convictions about how you handle it—a new wine skin.

Once you get a new paradigm, your finances can increase and stretch to any amount. Now you'll be able to handle money without going broke and wasting it. Get a new perspective on money and show God that He can trust you with the little paycheck you get at the little job you have, as well as the little investments you have. When you are able to do right with a little money, you can also do right with a lot! But as long as your paradigm stays in the same old place, no matter how much new money you make, you will mismanage a six-figure salary the exact same way you mismanage a five-figure one. Jesus says good or bad, the way you handle a little is the same way you will handle a lot. Stop fooling yourself into thinking you will do *anything* differently if your income suddenly goes from a little to a lot, because you're just going to manage it exactly the same way. The way you waste $45,000 a year is the *exact* same way you would waste $450,000 a year, or even $4,500,000. It's not your *money* that needs to change—it's *you*!

Day 25

"Train Up a Child"

During my childhood and youth, I was never thoroughly taught how to handle money. My first perception about money was that it was simply meant to be spent and used to get the things you wanted. I wasn't taught the basic rudiments of money management. When I was a young adult, though, my mother bought me a book by a financial guru named Suze Orman. Although I had never really heard of her at the time, I discovered she has written many books on the subject matter of finances. I am appreciative of my mother for getting me that book because I learned a great deal about finances that I never knew at the time and wished I had learned much earlier in life before becoming an adult. Yet from this experience I discovered that it's never too late to learn, nor is it ever too early to teach. As adults, it's never too late to acquire the knowledge needed to become financially free or to improve our financial state.

But on the flip side, we must also realize that one of the biggest favors we can do for our children is teach them about money and instill wise management practices in their minds as early as possible. Proverbs 22:6 says, "Train up a child the way he should go, and when he is old he will not depart from it." We have an obligation to learn—both for ourselves and for our children. We can't teach what we haven't first learned ourselves. But when we do learn, we have an obligation to teach, train, initiate, and provide discipline.

We can't keep letting Visa, Discover, MasterCard, collection agencies, and FICO be the training sources for our kids when it comes to financial management. Those involve often long years of painful lessons (Personally, Discover was my first teacher, and it was a painful lesson. She introduced me to late fees, interest rates, FICO, Equifax, Transunion, and everything else. I paid a lot for the lesson she gave me). Instead, we should train them by providing them with financial discipline and insight we wish we would have received as young children so that we could have been ready for the financial world once we entered it.

Training up a child the way he should go doesn't just mean to spiritually train them. It doesn't just entail teaching your child manners or acceptable social behaviors. Rather, it means that we train them in every capacity they need to be taught in order to successfully navigate through life as an adult when they are on their own. This includes financial training. Teach them to invest now, save now, earn different streams of income now, start a business now, be content now, think long term now, and avoid debt now! If you train them to do this now, when they get older they will not depart from the discipline you gave them as a child.

Day 26

"Who's the Master: God or Gold?"

One of the ways we mess up with God involves how we perceive our money. Many of us are so enslaved to our possessions and wealth that money is our god. In fact, we serve money more than we serve God Himself, even going so far as to rob God of the sacred tithe, which is 10% of our earned income, because we want as much of our money for ourselves as possible.

But the worst thing we can do is try to replace God with our money. Jesus taught in Matthew 6:24 that we cannot serve God and money because we will love one and hate the other. We would be willing to sacrifice ourselves for one of them and completely forego the other. God should be the source of our love—the one for whom we are willing to sacrifice our time, comfort, and other things. When it comes to money, however, it seems as if God becomes the object of our hate. Rather than sacrificing ourselves for God, we completely do without Him while making constant sacrifices to amass more and more money. Yet we must not let our desire for money become greater than our desire for God.

The children of Israel learned this difficult lesson in Exodus 32. They had just escaped Egyptian slavery with great wealth. God arranged for them to leave with gold and silver they collected from many of the Egyptian people. But as soon as they reached the wilderness, the Bible teaches that they took the gold they had, melted it down, reshaped it into a calf, and began to worship it as their god. After taking the wealth God made possible for them to acquire, they started worshipping it! They made sacrifices for it, gave it credit for how far they had come, and depended on it to take them even further. As you might imagine, this greatly displeased God.

It's a bad thing when we try to replace God with our goods. When we depend on our gold (i.e., money) because of our unwillingness to depend on God, it's not spiritually healthy. No matter what our branch of faith may be, God is never pleased when we make sacrifices for our gold that we won't make for Him as our God.

God doesn't mind us having wealth! He gave wealth to Israel because He wanted them to have all the gold they could carry. But He became angry when they took their financial blessing and made it a greater focal point for them than He. Likewise, God has no problem with your acquisition of as much wealth as your heart desires. He wants you to be as wealthy as you can be as long as you do the right thing with the wealth you have—as long as you honor Him with the wealth He has allowed you to get your hands on and don't value your money more than you value Him as your God. So be careful not to suddenly develop a spiritually dangerous view concerning your wealth. You can't serve two masters. As you seek out financial freedom, possess money, but make sure that you're only serving God, and not your money.

Day 27

"Rich in Deeds"

There are numerous rich people in this world, and conversely, there are plenty of people who aren't rich, but are presently striving for the financial status of having amassed great wealth—that place where they have no financial worries concerning the way they have already previously determined their desire to live their lives. That's what being rich really means. By definition, it means "plentiful." It doesn't mean having a certain amount of money, even though having ten million dollars would be nice! Rather, being rich simply means having plenty of money to live the lifestyle you have determined you want to live.

But as good as that sounds, being rich as a Christian comes with great responsibilities. If you fail to use your earthly riches responsibly in this life, it can cost you in the next life. In 1 Timothy 6:17, Paul instructed Timothy to warn rich people in the church not to be prideful because of their wealth, or place their hopes in their riches because of the uncertainty of wealth. Instead, he said they must put their hope in God, who supplies real riches. He told Timothy to teach rich Christians not to be so focused on being rich in money, but to also focus on being rich in good deeds.

Again, there is nothing wrong with being rich. God doesn't have an issue with His people having wealth. The problem lies when we're rich only in wealth but not in works. The more money we have, the more opportunity and responsibility we have to be a blessing to others here and there. In fact, Paul said to Timothy, "Tell them to be ready to distribute," because to whom much is given much more will be required.

We can't keep looking straight ahead at the stop lights when there are homeless people on the corner needing our financial generosity. We must be ready to distribute and give to others out of our plenty. We must not let our money go to our heads to the point we think that we're better than those suffering economic struggles. Instead, we should be willing to share our possessions with the less fortunate, the left out, and the left behind so they can have what we ourselves have.

If you are a rich Christian, which simply refers to a person who has more than enough for their personal needs and wants, God expects you to be charitable and give to those who can't help themselves. Donate to charities that assist the less fortunate and the oppressed. According to Paul, the reason you should do this is to ensure a certain exalted state of happiness and honor in heaven for yourself. You lay up treasures for yourself in eternity when you give a portion of your riches to those who need a blessing. As you pursue the necessary wealth that you deem necessary to live the life you desire to live, make sure not to use all of your wealth exclusively on you, but to fund some of your good works towards those who live a life in sharp contrast to your own. In other words, use some of your riches to help others.

Day 28

"Protect Yourself From Greed"

In Luke 12:15 Jesus advises that we guard ourselves against greed because life is *not about* how much stuff we have. I would add that it's also not about the *kind* of stuff we have, or if the stuff we have is the *latest* stuff. We get so entrapped financially trying to define ourselves by the things we accumulate and/or that in which we indulge. Greed, the "passion of wanting," causes us to make a lot of *senseless* decisions with our money. We want it, so we get it without considering the impact our "want" will have on our overall financial state. Therefore, we discover greed operates more out of want than out of wisdom, which leads to poverty or simply struggling financially.

This is the reason Jesus tells us to "guard" ourselves. In the Greek, this word means "to protect yourself from." If you don't protect yourself from the spirit of wanting—wanting this, that, this much, that much, this brand, that brand, this kind, that kind—you will remain broke, busted, and disgusted. So, make *wisdom* the supervisor of your wealth. Protect yourself and your wealth from being managed by your wants. Life is *not about* possessing your wants. This means you can have the big, impressive house that you can't afford to live in, the luxury car you can't afford to drive, the clothes you can't afford to wear, and the gadgets you can't afford to own, and *still* be living an unfulfilled, shallow, and meaningless life. Life is not about *things*, so stop investing the bulk of your wealth on things! Discover the true meaning of life itself, as well as *your unique* life, and I promise you will find out that you won't need to spend a whole lot of money on things to fulfill that definitive scope of your life.

Day 29

"You Can Learn A lot From an Ant"

When I was a little boy, I used to enjoy this commercial promoting seat belt safety. The ad would utilize walking talking car crash dummies that would always wear seat belts during test crashes for newly designed cars. The dummies would never get in a car without securing their seatbelts. Even though they would get banged up in the test crashes, they would always walk away alive. The campaign ad simply said, "You can learn a lot from a dummy!"

Not only can we learn a lot from a dummy, but we can learn a lot even from an ant as well—especially when it comes to handling our personal wealth. Solomon teaches us in Proverbs 6:6-9 that we need to be wise and consider the ways of the ant. The word "consider" in the original Hebrew means to "advise oneself." He recommends that we allow the ways of the ant to advise us in our own ways.

Solomon notes that the ant stores up bread during harvest time so that it can survive the upcoming winter. The ant saves some of the resources it gains, and puts them in a place where it can access them when they're desperately needed. Now, if we allow this analogy to advise us financially, it would communicate to us the wisdom of not consuming all the money that we have coming in, but rather taking a percentage of it and putting it in a place where we can access it when emergencies occur. Like the ant, we must exercise wisdom by anticipating tough times ahead.

Tough times come around for us all. When they come, however, a very small percentage of people are prepared to handle them. Most people are completely ill-prepared financially when winter-like times roll around; but not those who are like the ant. These people understand the importance of having a winter savings account (i.e., emergency savings account) sufficiently supplied with anywhere from $1,000 to $2,000 in it at all times that they absolutely *do not touch* until winter comes in its full effect.

Ants don't store bread during the summer and then nibble from it during the fall. Instead, they store it and access it *only* when winter comes. Because of this discipline of the ant, it never dies of hunger during the winter, but always survives because it was adequately prepared. We can learn a lot from the ant here. Let's not consume all of our money as soon as we get it in. But rather, let's take some of our financial harvest to store up for the winter—for chronic sickness, retirement, untimely death, unexpected emergencies, appliance failures, natural disasters, and benevolence for family members or friends. Be wise as the ant, and store up some bread now so that you can survive harsher times later.

Day 30

"Seek Wisdom"

If God came to you and told you to ask Him for anything, what would you ask for? Would you ask to be a millionaire or a billionaire? Would you wish to be famous? Would you ask to be the most powerful person in the world? Or would you ask for God to make all of your enemies pay for what they have done to you? I am willing to bet my right arm that the first or second thing that *did not* come to your mind was asking God to make you wiser!

Now this is something that probably will never happen for any of us. God will likely never ask us to wish for anything and He will give it to us, but for some reason He presented this genie-ish opportunity to King Solomon. In 2 Chronicles 1:7-12, God gave Solomon the opportunity to wish for anything he wanted, and Solomon took full advantage of this once-in-a-lifetime chance. The Bible says that he asked God for wisdom, which even seemed to surprise God. God responded to Solomon that he could have asked for the top three or four things He normally gets prayer requests from most people for: to be rich, to be famous, to live a long time, or to destroy his enemies. God said, "But instead, you asked for wisdom and knowledge." Solomon was wise enough to ask for a keen sense of rationality rather than prosperity, popularity, or longevity.

In response, God chose to give Solomon, in addition to the wisdom he asked for, prosperity and popularity. God decided that He could trust Solomon with prosperity because of the level of rationality he would acquire. Don't miss that: God *gave* Solomon wealth because he sought wisdom! If all you seek is wealth, your lack of wisdom will be a liability to your wealth. You will squander your money and lose it, or simply not understand what to do with it to make it grow or to best utilize it. But when you seek wisdom, wealth will come, and you'll know how to handle it.

There are different genres of wisdom, but I'm talking about financial wisdom here. If you seek to acquire financial wisdom to learn how investments work, how to be disciplined with money, and so on, God will allow wealth to come to you because He will know He can trust you with financial prosperity. So, in all of your pursuits, get financial wisdom, knowledge, and understanding—and then wealth will come.

Day 31

"Don't Be Evil"

Are you guilty of taking out a loan or borrowing money from someone or some established entity and not paying back what you borrowed? This includes swiping your credit card to make purchases and maxing out your card, but not paying your card completely off. Are you guilty of knowing you owe people or companies, but you duck and dodge their calls whenever they try to reach out to you to make payment arrangements with you for what you actually owe? I've been guilty of this myself. I have ignored calls and voice mails, as well as trashed physical mail and deleted e-mails from those trying to collect the money that I was obligated to pay back. In my younger days, I even allowed delinquent accounts to go into collection and let them sit there on my credit until they fell off. I was determined not to pay the hefty debt balances I owed, which included interest and other fees. Perhaps you are doing this today.

But I discovered this is not a good character trait for a person of faith. God doesn't condone such behaviors. Even if you are not a religious person, you must agree that this still indicates poor integrity and is very unethical. Psalm 37:21 declares, "An evil person borrows and never pays back." Today we would say, "An evil person swipes their credit card and never pays off their credit balance." Allow me to use some synonymous word for "evil" and see if this hits home. A *wicked* person borrows student loan money but never pays it back. A *criminal* borrows for an auto loan but never pays it all back. An *immoral* person borrows for a mortgage but never pays it all back. A *foul* person borrows money from a friend but never pays back what he or she borrowed. A *horrible* person uses a store's credit but doesn't make good on what they used to make store purchases.

You get the picture now. You are considered an evil, wicked, immoral, foul, horrible person to refuse to pay off your debts. This is not a good representation of people of faith, or of those who desires to maintain a wholesome and honest image. You don't want to have this type of reputation. At least I don't think you do! Therefore, you should strive to the best of your ability to repay that which you owe. You will be considered a respectable, lovely, fair, honorable, and ethical person when you stop avoiding to pay back what you rightfully owe.

Day 32

"Store Up or Gulp Down?"

We have talked before about the danger of being consumers; those who simply waste their resources by spending recklessly. You can always look at a person's life to know if she/he is a consumer or conserver. Is this person the type who spends as much as possible of what they get their hands on, or are they the type that save as much as possible of what they get their hands on? The NIV translation of Proverbs 21:20 declares that "the wise store up choice food and olive oil, but fools gulp theirs down." Another version says that "precious treasure and oil is in the house of the wise, but fools consume them." In other words, wise people store up their wealth, while fools gulp down theirs. Some people have nothing to show for all the finances they have been privileged to make because they've consumed it all.

Which person are you? Do you store up, or gulp down? Are you a consumer, or are you more of a conserver? It's wise to stop gulping so much of your wealth and start storing it up for later times. You will look foolish when you really need it but you have nothing to meet the needs that you have, because instead of saving it, you've already spent it!

Day 33

"Put a little to the side"

In 1 Corinthians 16:2, Paul taught the members of this New Testament church in Corinth how to financially prepare to contribute to the offering he would be collecting to assist the poor in Jerusalem. He simply told them to put a little to the side every week in order to save up for the special offering: "On the first day of every week, each one of you should set aside a sum of money in keeping with his income, saving it up, so that when I come no collections will have to be made."

Now, even though this is just the advice he gives the church to prepare for the benevolence offering, this can equally translate to our personal lives. Notice how Paul advises them to save money in proportion to their own individual incomes, because everyone should save what they can according to what they make. You can only do what you can do. If you would like to save more money, you should do either one of two things, if not both: 1) reduce your expenses; or 2) generate another stream of income. Until then, save what you are able to save, whether it's $100 a week, $500 a month or simply $10 a pay period. Whatever it is, make it your business to regularly set something aside.

Paul advises his audience to set money aside every Sunday (i.e., the first day of the week). I'm not sure why he suggests Sunday, but it's irrelevant. The point is that he recommends they adopt a systematic savings routine. Likewise, saving needs to be an intentional financial practice that should be a normal part of your financial management. Saving should already be included in your plans of what to do with your money when you get it.

Any money that hits my hand, the first thing I always think about is how much of it I can save. Now, I wasn't born this way. I had to grow into this mindset. It took years of practice until it finally became a habit for me. Now it's fortunately a lifestyle. This is the goal you want to grow towards—continually saving a sum of money until it's no longer your habit, but your lifestyle. Habits can be broken, but lifestyles are ingrained within your very being. When a habit becomes your lifestyle, it becomes your mindset, your standard, or your new normal. Whether you're saving for your retirement, emergency fund, college for your kids, vacations, or any other special items, regularly put a sum of money aside so that your funds can be ready when that time comes around for you.

Day 34

"The *if's* of Life"

As I write this, I am attempting to finish this book. My church and I have just finished our 40-day financial fast journey, and together with my wife, we have been able to save thousands of dollars. I've been preaching to my church for the last few weeks about some of the biblical insights I have been sharing here with you. I've also been giving them many statistics about financial matters as it relates to American life today. One of those stats that I shared repeatedly was that the average unexpected emergency can be taken care of with $1,000 or less, but that shockingly 69% of Americans don't have a savings account with at least $1,000 in it. I was encouraging my members at Piney Grove to save their own money to avoid having to use credit cards or payday loans to take care of their own unexpected emergencies, because whether you like it or not, they will happen.

It's funny that seven days after I preached about these principles, those unexpected emergencies started happening to me! But my wife and I weren't worried because we had saved up for such times. Within seven days after the fast, our built-in microwave died, and both of our cars needed to go into the shop. I called for a repairman to come out and fix the microwave that Friday because we had a big family dinner planned for Easter. I had to put one car in the shop that Saturday, and the very next day, Easter Sunday, we went to load the truck up to head home after two powerful services, when one of our staff persons turned the key to start the truck . . . and nothing. The truck wouldn't even turn over or make a sound. We all assumed it was the starter, but we still realized that we had to get the truck towed to the exact same shop that was working on our other car. After it was all said and done, because of the fast, we had more than enough money to get both cars fixed and back on the road. Thank God we saved when we did because our planning helped us during the time we experienced a transportation famine.

I once heard a person say, "In the middle of the word l*if*e is the word 'if.' " What are you going to do *if* this happens or *if* that happens? When thinking about life, we need to be prepared as much as possible for as many of the *ifs* of life as possible. This is what Joseph was talking about when he advised the Pharaoh of Egypt to save resources for the next seven years of abundance, so the nation could survive the seven years of famine that would follow. In Genesis 41:34-36, Joseph presents a seven-year savings plan in order for them to save in the good times so that they may survive in the bad times.

My wife and I were able to handle that period of going without both of our cars for a few days and being able to get them both fixed because we saved when times were good. We were prepared for "if" the microwave dies, "if" a part in the car needs fixing, and "if" the truck suddenly dies. We were prepared for at least three of life's "ifs." This experience encouraged us to continue to save, because other unexpected emergencies are coming. If they are coming for us, surely they are coming for you as well! So you need to use this time to prepare for *life*. Prepare for as many of its *ifs* as you possibly can.

Day 35

"...and It was Good"

Do me a favor. Close your eyes and take the next 60 seconds to imagine your ideal financial world. Take longer if you need to. What did you imagine? Did it look good to you? Were you debt free and prosperous? Were you vacationing and enjoying life? Did you have some of the things you've always wanted? Did you look stressed about your money situation? I'm sure you imagined a financial world that was a joy for you to live in! Well, guess what? Just about all you imagined, if you plan right and operate in discipline, you can have—if not all of it, certainly to some extent.

You *can* create your ideal financial world. However, creating this world that you have imagined in your mind is a process. The fast is almost over, but you still have a lot of work to do. Just don't allow yourself to get frustrated with all you still have left to do. Rather, change your perspective, and celebrate all that you have already done!

Even if we haven't read the Bible all the way through, nearly *every one* of us has cracked open the first page and read Genesis 1. There, we read that God moved to create His ideal world. He took that which was no more than a picture in His mind and turned that ideal world into a reality. Take note how God created His ideal world. He worked on one or two things at a time. He did it day by day. Accomplishing one objective at a time, He got closer and closer to seeing His ideal world materializing. With each achieved objective or goal, He took the time to celebrate Himself and what He had done so far by calling it "good." Notice that he never considered all he had left to do, or frustrated himself by fretting over what was still left undone. Rather, he took in what had been successfully achieved, and He celebrated it.

As you seek to create your ideal world, take the time to celebrate what you have done. Be proud of every bill paid, every debt cleared out, every dollar saved, every savings goal met, every investment started, every point your credit score improves, etc. Don't worry about all you still have left to do and how much money you still have left to save. Instead, celebrate yourself! What have you done already that's more than you had accomplished yesterday, last week, last month, or even last year? Celebrate those things and continue to build your ideal financial world one day or one goal at a time. If you stay consistent with the building process, the day will come when you can consider just how far you have come, and enjoy the work of your hands.

Day 36

"Use your Ability"

A couple of days ago we briefly talked about two ways to increase your ability to save more cash: 1) reduce your expenses; or 2) generate another stream of income. Let's focus now on generating another stream of income. Are you guilty of trying to navigate through life on just one financial stream? Is your 9 to 5 job your only income stream? Let me ask you this: what are you going to do if that stream dries up? I think it's safe to say that living on one stream may be working for you at the moment, but just having one stream alone isn't the wisest course available to you. Certainly, some of your streams will not be as large as others, but you do need something else flowing besides that one means of income coming in.

Yes, we need to reduce our spending. Yes, we need to get out of debt. Yes, we need to invest. Yes, we need to save. But we also need to consider creating another financial stream. If you are thinking this is impossible for you, remember Deuteronomy 8:18, "Remember the Lord your God, for it is he that gives you the power to get wealth." That word "power" in the biblical Hebrew language means "capacity, means, or ability." One of the meanings for the word "get" means "to bring forth." In other words, "God has given you the capability, the means, and the ability to bring forth wealth." And that capability isn't all bottled up in the one thing you do right now. That ability is much more extensive than most of us are utilizing right now. For the most part, we are guilty of failing to maximize our God-given ability to bring forth hundreds, thousands, if not maybe even millions of dollars!

Ask yourself, "What can I do to bring forth more wealth? What can I offer? What service can I provide? What can I create? What can I come up with? What can I invest in? Who can I partner up with to go into a side business to produce more wealth?" There is more wealth in you; you just need to use what you already have in you to produce it and bring it forth. For the most part, money isn't just going to come to you. Instead, you have to use what God gave you and produce it. Make wreaths, bake cakes, cater in your spare time, do some public speaking, write a book, counsel, etc. Tap into yourself until you discover that capability or idea within you that, when unleashed, will bring about more wealth for you and become another financial stream that you and your family can enjoy.

Day 37

"Be Diligent"

Creating that next stream of income is something that is beneficial to you, but it's also something that doesn't come easy. It takes work, grit, focus, and determination. You can't be lazy and expect wealth to come forth for you. Proverbs 10:4 echoes this as well: "A slack hand causes poverty, but the hand of the diligent makes rich." A "slack hand" refers to a lazy person. Generally, lazy people don't ever know prosperity, but rather only poverty or even mediocrity.

The other alternative to the slack hand is the diligent hand. This is a person marked by determination, will power, and resolve. This individual has sheer tenacity in that he doesn't shy away from challenges. He doesn't walk away or quit because something is hard to accomplish or requires a lot of time and effort to achieve. This is a person who sticks with the complete process, trusting that if they puts something in, they will surely get much more out.

You must be diligent to become financially free. You have to keep at it! You will oftentimes take three steps forward and then four steps backwards, but you must have the determination required to overcome that four-step digression with a five-step progression, followed by another one-step advance. Diligence is the key to get out of debt, start your business, create your ideal financial world, be financially set when you get ready to retire, and create another stream of income.

Whatever you desire to do financially that will lead to prosperity for you, you must learn to have a diligent hand. With a diligent hand, you can't fail financially. Your diligence will keep you on top of your financial empire and in control of every boardroom decision that needs to be made to keep your personal money matters healthy. You are the boss of your Fortune 500 company. You must run your personal finances as if it is a corporate business, because it is, if you learn to see it that way. Your personal financial life will rise or fall based on which type of CEO you pan out to be—one with a slack hand, or one with a diligent hand.

Day 38

"Persistence Pays Off"

"Ambition is the path to success; persistence is the vehicle you arrive in." This is a quote I ran across one day that highlights the value of the unbeatable attribute called persistence. Persistence is defined as a firm or stubborn continuance in a course of action in spite of difficulty or opposition. Don't miss that! It is a stubborn, adamant, tenacious prolongation down a certain path despite the complications associated with the path. Being persistent means that you will keep going and going, no matter what you have to go through to get what you're after. It means that there isn't any "quit" in you; instead, you are ready to sacrifice your last breath to pursue what you have fixed your eyes upon. It's a type of determination that will not succumb to anything but death itself.

Persistence is an attribute that you must have to know success at every level and in every arena. Remember what the quote says: *It drives you to success.* This involves more than just making a determined effort, because every determined effort doesn't promise a desired result. Just because you seriously tried doesn't guarantee that your attempt will turn out to be fruitful. Success does not normally happen during the initial effort. More often than not, success occurs because of persistent effort.

Jesus once told a parable in Luke 18:1-5 about a widowed woman who was persistent. She kept visiting a certain judge seeking justice concerning her situation, and he kept denying her. Jesus says that the woman kept going to the judge so much that eventually he said to himself, "Because this woman keeps bothering me, I will see that she gets justice so that she doesn't eventually wear me out with her coming!" In this story, Jesus was emphasizing the element of persistence. Vividly portraying how some things do not happen as a result of initial effort, but rather as a result of persistent effort.

The reason you may not have successfully created that next income stream is that your effort may have been authentic, but it wasn't persistent. The reason you haven't drastically reduced your debt is because your effort was sincere, but it wasn't persistent. You never accomplished those key financial goals you wanted to reach because even though you put forth a legitimate effort, you didn't continue to put forth a *persistent* effort. Anybody can try, and most people can even try again. But it takes a particular kind of person to keep trying again and again and again and again. That's where real success is mostly found—in that audacious attempt, even after previous attempts have already succumbed to multiple failures.

So, if you want to attain a financially successful place, you must be persistent in every part of your financial life. Persist in the decisions you make, and the business deals you agree to. Be persistent in building important relationships, seeking out growth opportunities, and sticking with your plan. You can have ambition, but ambition alone is not enough. Effort alone is not enough. Along with these, you need persistence to drive you down the path towards financial success.

Day 39

"Don't Look Back"

How does it feel to have nearly completed your first 40-day financial fast? I hope that this fast has helped to change the way you see money and the way you handle money, as well as assisted you with being well on your way to pursuing the financial freedom you have desired for so long. I pray that this fast has been useful in leading you out of the poverty mindset, along with delivering you from the destructive ways that you have been so comfortably practicing for most, if not all, of your life as a steward of your personal finances.

Now it's time for you to finally come all the way out of this poor stewardship of your wealth. It's time to completely separate yourself from the destructive mentality that has governed the way you have handled your money all this time. But as you make your way out of this poverty cycle that you have been a part of for so long—this paycheck-to-paycheck lifestyle, this fiscally irresponsible routine— let me warn you to beware the danger of drifting back into those same typical poor financial management habits and wasteful, loss-making, unprofitable stewardship practices that you have employed for so many years.

Don't be like the fool of Proverbs 26:11, which says, "As a dog returns to its vomit, so fools repeat their foolishness." By now you should see that many of the things you have been doing with your wealth was just that—pure foolishness. The question is, are you foolish enough to return to those same foolish ways, or are you wise enough to keep moving in the ways of wisdom financially? This is an important question that you need to seriously consider because many people have been on their way out of a toxic situation, only to mess up and let the urge to return to their vomit get the best of them.

This is why Jesus told His disciples in Luke 17:32, "Remember Lot's wife." This woman was on her way out of a destructive place, but she allowed her urge for the lifestyle she was being pulled away from to get the best of her. Like a dog returning to its vomit, she looked back and it destroyed her. One of the most significant takeaways we can glean from learning all that transpired with this woman is that you can't ever progress into something better for yourself when you keep revisiting habits that are unhealthy and downright destructive.

You must learn how to completely walk away from the things that are destroying you, and never look back. Once you get out of debt, never look back! The moment you become financially stable for the first time in your adult life, never look back! The first time you get your credit score at a respectable level, never look back! When you get to the place where you don't have to use a credit card if you don't want to, take out a payday loan, or borrow from someone else because you now have your own money to use, never look back! Resist the urge to go back to your vomit! Once you get all the bad financial habits out of your system, such as living from paycheck to paycheck, being broke all the time, robbing Peter to pay Paul, and being a complete consumer, *never* return back to it! Don't be a fool! Refuse to return to the same old financial foolishness, because it's out of you now. Instead, keep moving toward financial freedom.

Day 40

"Stay on Your Feet"

All right! It's day 40! You made it! Wow, what a journey, huh? Let me be the first to say that I am extremely proud of you. This has been a long, hard detox, but you trusted the process and let it reveal all the things it needed to reveal to you. Now you are ready to continue down this healthy path of financial freedom! Even though this is day 40, it's just the beginning for you as a better steward of your wealth. Remember, this book was designed to just get you on this very long path to travel. Now that you have come this far, I want to encourage you with a very important piece of wisdom for our last journal entry.

In John 5, Jesus met a man who couldn't walk. He was on a stretcher and had been that way for almost forty years. However, Jesus healed him, and the man was able to get back on his feet. The detail that catches my attention is that later, Jesus bumped into the man again and told him this in verse 14: "Look at you! You are standing on your own two feet now. Now don't do the things you once were doing anymore or something *worse* may happen to you!"

Doing this financial fast for the past 40 days I'm sure has indeed help you get on your feet financially. And in no time you'll be well on your way to enjoying the freedom that accompanies standing on your own two feet; no longer needing people or systems to carry

135

you. No longer will you need a credit card to carry you, a friend to spot you $20 until payday, or somebody to look out for you because you can't financially look out for yourself. No longer will you have to make payment arrangements for your utility bills. No longer will you only have enough money to go on special trips, but not enough money to enjoy the special trip that you're on. You will be able to freely stand on your own two feet.

But be careful! This fast is not meant to get you on your feet so you can go *right* back to doing those things that financially crippled you to begin with. Instead, it's meant to deliver you—to get you free and keep you free so that you won't have to be dependent on other things or people to keep carrying you. So Jesus' words are very important. He's basically saying, "Don't go back and start doing the same things that crippled you." And so I say to you, don't go back to being financially sinful or something worse will happen to you! You will find yourself right back in financial debt, bad off, in a terrible place during your retirement years, and dependent on others to carry you once again.

I don't know about you, but I like it better on my feet. I don't like being in a place where I'm stuck and limited because I don't have anybody to carry me, feel sorry for me, or give me a financial handout. I don't like being dependent on a paycheck to get me through the next two weeks of the month, or always having more month left than I have money left. I like being on my feet; free to move about financially whenever and wherever I want to go. And Jesus shows us that once we get on our feet, staying on our feet comes with some responsibility. We are responsible for making sound financial decisions that keep us on our feet, instead of those that cripple us and send us right back into dependency—even putting us in far worse shape financially than we've ever been. So, do yourself a favor and stay on your feet!

"Wherefore gird up the loins of your mind..." I Peter 1:13

The imagination is one of the most powerful gifts given to man by God. However, it is believed by a number of psychologists and even neurologist that this most powerful gift is only really used by most from the age of 2 until about age 7. Meaning that the average person only consistently imagines for about 5 years of their lives. Psychologist note that the reason for this is because somewhere after the 2nd grade, for some reason, it becomes socially unacceptable to imagine, & children are persuaded against using their imaginations. Consequently, once a child becomes 6/7 years old, what is arguably one of the most powerful gifts given to man by God, goes from being greatly encouraged, to being greatly discouraged. And the same children who were once full of imagination, tragically grow up to become adults with absolutely no imagination at all. They become adults who fail to use their imaginative ability.

Albert Einstein is quoted in saying, *"Your imagination is your preview of life's coming attractions."* Meaning, you determine what's next for your life by constantly previewing it first in your own mind. Proverbs 23:7 agrees by saying, *"as a man thinketh in his heart, so is he."* 'Thinketh' is an old English word that basically means *continues to think*. So the way a person continues to think is the way that person's life eventually becomes. You see, imagining is where our creative potential lies. We can sculpt, shape, reshape, design & enrich our lives just by simply imagining. Take into account that everything in which exist today that has revolutionized the way we live, is a direct result of someone else's imagination. We have planes that fly thousands of miles through the air today b/c of someone's imagination. The cars we drive, the trains we ride in, the TV's we watch, the phones that we voice, video and text communicate with, the boats that we cruise the oceans & seas in, the internet that we use are all direct results of someone's imagination. Our world has rapidly progressed and changed, NOT by coincidence, but because people dared to imagine, and were brave enough to unleash their imaginations! And if unleashed imaginations have the power to change an entire world, transform an entire civilization, & advance a whole generation, how beneficial could it be for us personally if we intentionally started imagining things for our own lives? What would our lives look like if we really imagined, and then unleashed our imaginations?

My wife, Precious Williams likes to say, *"Imagine your life without excuses; now live that life."* Form a mental picture in your mind of what your life would look like if you never made an excuse or allowed an excuse to get in your way, & then unleash that imagination into your real life. I would encourage you to imagine your life debt free, and start living that life. Imagine your life free of financial worry, and start living that life. Imagine your life financially free! Being able to live life on your terms, and not dictated by your next paycheck! Imagine it, and LIVE THAT LIFE! Gather up all of your thinking ability, and muster up every imaginative brain cell you can recruit to see yourself financially free. And once you start seeing it in your mind, start employing every discipline, strategy, idea, concept and principle discussed in this book to turn your imagination into realization!

Made in the USA
Columbia, SC
26 June 2018